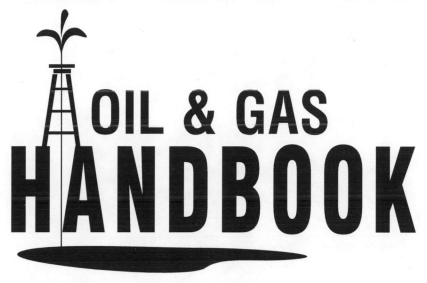

OIL & GAS HANDBOOK

A ROUGHNECK'S GUIDE TO THE UNIVERSE

WILL PETTIJOHN P.E.C.

authorHOUSE®

AuthorHouse™
1663 Liberty Drive
Bloomington, IN 47403
www.authorhouse.com
Phone: 1-800-839-8640

Published by AuthorHouse 2/23/2012

ISBN: 978-1-4685-4531-9 (sc)
ISBN: 978-1-4685-4532-6 (hc)
ISBN: 978-1-4685-4533-3 (e)

Library of Congress Control Number: 2012901301

Preface;

More times than I can remember, I've heard the term "If you want to do something badly enough, you can do it." I believe that's true, you can teach a nine year old kid quantum physics, if you make it interesting enough to keep his/her attention. Learning is all about attitude, if you interest someone, you can make them remember anything.

In this book, you'll learn the BASIC order for performing the tasks of a roughneck. As we cover these steps, I caution you "Do not mistake these pages as your company's policies and Procedures." This is a general and practical set of instructions. Your company's policies may not agree with these some of these steps. In some cases, you will skip one or more of the steps mentioned in this book. As technology continues to improve our tasks each day; there are steps that are taken out or put in to protect you as an employee, and the environments as well. When you have a question about these steps and the chance of a conflict with your company's policies, look into your company's best practices and operations manual, or simply ask a supervisor. You may see several differences in the things that are discussed here and in your companies' policies and procedures. Again, this is simply a set of general instructions that may or may not be relevant to your tasks and the operations that you are involved in.

Remember this; we all begin at the same level as a roughneck and choose to learn from there. It is up to you and the company that you work for as to how far you are able to progress in this industry. As you learn each step, you will begin to finesse your own skills and become a more efficient employee. We will cover several aspects including rig move, basic rig equipment, extended rig equipment, vertical wells, horizontal wells and directional wells. There is a common misconception about the oil

& gas industry (also called the oilfield); it has been said that roughnecks are people that cannot learn a trade, that we are a breed of failures who can't keep a job in routine positions, such as a factory or other types of positions.

The oilfield can be a very lucrative career. Most of people that venture into the oilfield never do anything else for a living and choose this industry over other options. I have known men that have been in the coal industry for twenty or thirty years who are now in the oilfield and they love it. If you want to learn, you need to ask questions and pay attention to even the smallest of details. Remember; the more that you know, the better you'll be at anything you attempt.

This Book is dedicated to all Oil & Gas Professionals everywhere!

I'd like to make A special mention of; Jim Baker, Jim Tilley, Jim Howell, Dan Lindsey, Robert Dysart, Brian Dutton, Jean Trahan, Robert Guidroz, Bill Smith and my very good friend David Rodgers.

Thank you all for mentoring me and for being the men that you are.

CHAPTERS

CHAPTER 1

RIG MOVE & RIG UP

All oil or gas wells begin in the same place. We must have a drilling rig, a location and a drilling program to complete the operation of drilling an oil or gas well.

(**Location;** a permitted piece of property designed to support and maintain the Rig during normal drilling operations)

Once we have our location permitted and surveyed, it must then be designed for the type of rig that is going to move onto it. If your rig is a diesel electric, for example; you will probably need a much larger location than a double jackknife or single lay-down rig would need. These are three different types of rigs that we will cover later. If your Rig requires a reservoir or reserve pit, it should be ready and lined, before you arrive on location.

If your rig is a multi load rig, you will use several trucks to move the rig. Some rigs, such as an RD-20 or a Schramm rig are mounted onto a truck themselves and only require trucks to move their pipe trailers and equipment. We should have trucks on location early. You will see several different types of trucks, such as haul trucks, bed trucks, pole trucks "in some instances" and cranes and forklifts if necessary. These trucks will have their own operators and more than likely a swamper for each truck; swampers do the tying on and spotting.

You as a roughneck will more than likely need to help these people in tying onto and spotting the equipment as it is moved. If your rig is large enough to use several trucks, you will more than likely have one crew on the old location, loading out the equipment and one crew on the new location doing a spot in rig up.

(**Spot in rig up;** rigging up all that you can, as the rig is brought in that doesn't slow the rig move down)

You will need several tools, so ask your driller or tool pusher/ rig manager what tools you will need. Remember, the more you do without being told, the quicker you'll move up in this industry. You will be helping someone who knows where each load is to be placed. As the loads begin arriving, try and think about where they are supposed to go and be ready for them. For the most part, your rig will only go together one way. After you have rigged the Rig up once, you will know better where things are and supposed to be.

(Remember that everything you put together should be tight and ready to drill. If you put something together handy "hand tight" it looks tight and it may be missed later, some things that are pressurized during normal drilling operations and are not tight could result in an accident. So if you put it together, tighten it up; this will save valuable time and energy later, because it will already be done. And it also may prevent a horrific accident if it is done right the first time.)

In general, the first things that will arrive will be the substructure and several other loads at once, (mud tanks) also known as mud pits will come with the first loads. The substructure, draw works and other loads that will be used to put these together. First they will bring in the substructure and level it. The substructure is placed in the center of the location over the planned well-bore. The mud tanks are always placed at the back of location next to the reserve pit (if applicable) or reclamation tanks in other cases will be set up to receive the materials that will be removed from the earth during the drilling operations. Then they will bring in the shaker/ sand pit and set it into place. They will place it and adjust it according to the schematic of your rig. If your rig has a two tank system, they will bring in the settling/suction pit next. Unless your rig only has a one mud tank system which is becoming more common in many cases; then these two will serve the purpose of holding, treating and reclaiming the active drilling fluids during the drilling operations. This is where you come in; you will need to connect all of the hoses, risers and spreaders between the two tanks and install the walkway and handrails. After the pit/pits are set in, ask your supervisor if you need to put any handrails or anything else on top of them (remember to wear your harness if there is a chance of falling). Some mud tanks/pits have stationary handrails and others do not, it usually depends upon the height restrictions when mobilizing. You may also need to bolt down a de-sander/de-silter or shaker assembly and connect any hoses that would accompany them as well. These may be removed or they may stay on the mud tanks when mobilizing; depending on how tall your tanks are, some equipment must be removed for clearances under bridges and other low lying structures.

After the pits have been set in, a lot more will be happening. Your supervisor will let you know what you will be doing as the day progresses. Remember O.S.H.A. (the Occupational Safety & Health Administration) a federal safety and regulatory organization, has certain laws that you must comply with. So you'll need to remember the safety rules that your company has set forth in accordance to the regulations and made you aware of. We will cover a few of the O.S.H.A. rules as we get further in depth. For instance, any person that is 4 feet or more off of the ground (at their foot position) must be tied off 100% using a fall protection apparatus. This is usually a full body harness, if you have to wear a full body harness, it should be fitted to your body frame and inspected daily for wear and tear. After you have observed the safety rules of O.S.H.A. and your company, it's time to get to work.

During the process of installing the mud tanks and hooking them together, the substructure will be set in and leveled. If you are going to be putting the substructure together, you will have to use a few tools. You may need to drive pins into the different components to secure them together. You may have to use a level, to insure the substructure is level and drill stable. This is usually done while the pusher has the trucks raise or lower to adjust it and level it by placing boards under the sides or front and back. The substructure is the base of the operation; this is what holds everything else above it. A substructure is rated for depth and weight by certain qualities that are built into the structural steel. These range from shallow hole substructures to more than forty thousand feet substructures and this is regulated by mandatory periodic inspections called category (CAT) inspections. After the substructure is now spotted in place, level and ready to receive the other components, you will have to get with your supervisor to find out where you'll be working. There are several different types of substructures. There are hydraulic slingshot substructures, box type substructures, double box substructures and even pony substructures. You may receive two sides and several components that will be placed in the middle to connect the two sides. These inner pieces are often called frogs, because they jump from one side to the other. You may see one large substructure on your rig. This type of substructure usually only has a rotary table that is removed for mobilization. The box on box type substructure usually has one main base substructure and then pony substructures that are placed under them to obtain a certain height requirement. This is usually to accommodate a blow out preventer configuration for the area that you'll be drilling in.

After the substructure has been put together and leveled, the derrick is ready to be installed; the crane or pole trucks will attach a cable or sling onto either end of it and maneuver it over the substructure where it is to be pinned onto the floor of the substructure. You will then line it up and drive your pins into the allotted pin holes. The derrick stand will be placed under the other end of the derrick. The trucks will lower the derrick onto the stand; this in turn, will release the trucks from the derrick, so they can continue to rig up. After pinning the derrick and releasing the trucks, one truck will raise the a-legs. After the a-legs are raised and pinned into place the blocks will be set onto the catwalk to be strung up with drilling line. The derrick is the large tower structure which stands in the air and houses the traveling blocks, or the track and top drive which will be installed after it is pinned to the substructure. The derrick is usually the only part of the rig you see in the air when the rig is noticed from a distance. The derrick is also called a mast, but the more common term in the oilfield is derrick. If your rig is a free block and tackle rig, then you will string the blocks and install the pick-up line (also called a bull line) at this point. If it is a top drive rig, then you will install the track that it will ride on and then string the blocks and install the bull line. The derrick keeps the blocks and drilling assembly in the center of the operation to distribute the weight of the drill string. The weight of the drill string can astonish some people who aren't used to dealing with weights such as that. A derrick is designed very carefully and is an engineering marvel.

On all rigs except truck mounted rigs, or hydraulic track rigs, you will install the draw works, also known as a draw tool. This is the winch on for the power end of the rig. There will be a large winch assembly with either mechanical motors or electrical components to power it and allow the blocks to be moved up or down when needed. In the instance of mechanical motors, they will be either attached to the draw works skid, or they will be separate and will be attached using chains which drive the torque converters which in turn power a clutch and then gears that operate the blocks. If your rig is a SCR (silicon-controlled rectifier) you will need to attach the electrical lines to provide the power source to the draw works. On an SCR rig, the difference is; the motors which power the gears are electric friction motors, instead of mechanical geared motors. These are often cleaner and less noisy rigs that are capable of a lot more horsepower. After all fuel lines, electrical lines and hydraulic lines have been ran to their proper place and tightened up to the motors or power source; then you can string your blocks and bull line, or install the top drive track for the blocks, with 6,8,10 or in some cases even12 lines; this will allow more or less string weight to be lifted by the blocks.

(**Example:** If your blocks have 5 sheaves, you could Rig up on 6, 8 or 10 lines)

The blocks may use 8 lines if the well is not going to be very deep. Most rigs use 10 to 12 lines if the blocks are capable to handle the weight and the blocks house enough sheaves. The more lines used, the slower the blocks will travel, but the more weight you're able to lift with the blocks. After you have strung the blocks, using the drilling line, then you will attach it to the draw works. Some rigs leave the blocks strung up when they move. These are usually the smaller rigs, but if it is an option, it makes it convenient and efficient for moving and rigging up. Different size rigs use different size drilling line and will also use a different number of lines running through the blocks. After you get the block or top drive rigged up, you should be ready to raise the derrick.

The next step is raising the derrick, with the exception of the truck mounted rigs that we discussed earlier, where the derrick is mounted permanently; this is not referring to the fixed truck rigs that scope up and down. The truck mounted rigs stay together and to raise the of derrick, you simply pull hydraulic levers. You can now perform the visual derrick inspection and weight stress test. The derrick inspection is a visual inspection, to insure that all safety pins, bolts, shackles and clevises are installed properly

(Note: If any piece of equipment is to be overhead, it must be approved to be used as an overhead device; secured using a safety pin assembly and a safety cable in the event that the safety pin should fail. This will insure that the equipment will not fall out of the derrick during the raising or drilling operations.)

The stress test is a company regulated test, as well as an API (American Petroleum Institute) standard test to be performed on the derrick at its heaviest and most stressful point. Once the derrick is raised off of the derrick stand, which is the most stressful point. The industry standard is @ 89° degrees or 6" for 20 minutes. This means, that you'll raise the derrick off of the derrick stand approximately 6" and hold it there for approximately 20 minutes. This places all of the weight on the pick-up line or bull line. The objective of this test is to prevent dropping the derrick in the event of a line failure. If the line fails, the derrick will only fall the distance that it is off of the stand and is less likely to hurt someone falling such a short distance.

A visual walk around inspection of these lines, sheaves and all other components should be performed before and during the stress test. Once the stress test is performed and all lines have passed, the derrick can then be raised and pinned into place and the rig up can be completed.

(Warning) do not stand under the derrick as it is being raised.

Anything could happen, causing the derrick to fall and crush you.

Even a new line can fail and cause the derrick to fall. Stay a safe distance away while you're watching all of the lines and keeping them from getting pinched or hung onto something during the raising process.

The next step, after the derrick is pinned and secured, is to begin bringing all of the floor equipment onto the rig floor. Such as the tongs, swivel, kelly, valves and miscellaneous tools needed. The tongs are going to be hung onto separate stationary cables attached to the derrick and counter weight buckets; these counterweights will assist in raising and lowering the tongs due to the extreme weight of them. The tongs are also attached to the derrick leg using a snub-line; this prevents the tongs from moving further than the desired position and causing serious injury when being used. The tongs are also hooked to a cable or chain from the draw-works; this is the power side of the tongs and will force the tongs in a desired direction to tighten or loosen the tubular as it is being placed into or removed from the drill string.

(**Tubular;** is a piece of threaded pipe, drill pipe/drill collar, casing, motor, sub etc.)

Now the (back yard) can be completely rigged up and prepared for the drilling operations. The back yard refers to everything that goes behind the rig. At this time, you will probably spot in the mud mumps, two if applicable, some rigs only use one mud pump and others use up to three. So you will have one, two or three of them to rig up and connect together, depending on how large your rig is and how deep you are drilling. Most rigs have tri-plex pumps; they use three swab pistons to pull in and expel the drilling fluid; which will give the desired volume and pressure will be needed to drill. After spotting the mud pumps, you will probably set in the rest of your back yard; such as a water tank, light plant/generator or SCR house, mud house (if applicable), a diesel tank and the other buildings that may also be on your well site.

All drilling rigs must have diesel, the diesel lines will have to be ran and hooked up to all components. Some rigs are diesel electric rigs; these rigs have an SCR house that distributes electricity to miscellaneous components instead of using a specific motor for each individual component. In this instance, an electric line is ran and attached to each component, with a variety of distribution panels in strategic places; this will allow one single large cable to be ran to the distribution panel and the smaller satellite cables will be ran to the many components from there.

On the power rigs, or compound rigs, this changes a bit. Power rigs, also called compound rigs, due to the oil storage reservoir it uses to lubricate the gears, will have a motor for each component such as the draw-works, mud pumps and even the generator. Even as the component has its own motor, it will still need diesel and more than likely air for the starter and clutch. On most power rigs; you will need 3 lines ran to each motor, one for diesel, one for air supply and one for the clutch actuation to engage the clutch from a remote panel. If lights are on the component, or it has an electric actuation solenoid, you will need to run an electric line to these motors as well.

SCR houses will need a diesel supply line, as they will run constantly; the diesel flow is being alternated between three or more motors, depending on which generators are running at one time. Each of these motors will have a large generator connected to them. This is the electricity that is supplied to the rig. Instead of air lines for clutch actuation, you will have an electric line to engage an electric motor in many different places on the rig. The designers simply replaced a mechanical component with an electrical drive system in this instance. SCR houses must stay at a very cool temperature to prevent the electrical components from overheating. SCR houses will have multiple air conditioners to keep it very cool inside. The application for a diesel electric rig is advantageous because of the horsepower and less intrusive nature of the electric rigs. The SCR rig it is not as loud as a conventional rig is; this application is perfect in the event that you are drilling near a home or community. These types of rigs are often used in cities to help avoid disturbing the public during the operations.

Some rigs are hydraulic, these rigs, are generally slow but powerful. The application of the hydraulic rig is the same as the SCR rig, but they require an HPU to provide the pressure to move components. HPU stands for hydraulic power unit. It is operationally sound but has its own set of issues. More than likely the rig floor will be the most tedious to rig up. Once you have rigged up the rig floor, the back yard all of the necessary lines, you will probably be rigging up the front yard. The cat-walk will more than likely have already been placed by this time because the blocks are usually set onto it to be strung up or placed for the derrick raising operations. Perhaps all that is left to be rigged up in the front yard is the pipe racks and drill collars/drill-pipe placed onto the racks and the accumulator should be rigged up as well.

After you have rigged up the front yard and completed all of the tasks of the rig up, the top drive, power swivel will be rigged up (if applicable). That is unless you are on a kelly rig, in that event, the kelly and independent swivel will be rigged up. The swivel is a component that allows rotation of the string while maintaining pressure on the string and well-bore. The swivel has an inlet thread half union; this is where you will hook up the kelly hose. The kelly hose is a high pressure hose which allows fluid or air to be pumped into the well-bore from pump or air compressor and then through the standpipe where it will go through the swivel and then down through the drill string.

The standpipe is a high pressure pipe assembly attached to and running the length of the derrick. It is then connected to the mud pumps through another high pressure hose called a vibrating hose, which is housed in the substructure. The swivel is set into the blocks, using the block hook. Swivels have a kelly beal that rests in the block hook, securing the swivel as it travels inside the derrick and holds the drill string weight. The kelly screws onto the swivel with an upper kelly valve also known as an upper kelly cock, or a crossover sub. The kelly is the hex pipe or square pipe that rests in the kelly bushings. The kelly bushings then set into the rotary table and are forced to turn using a sprocket drive coming from the draw works. The sprocket drive is connected to the draw-works using several chains and gears.

The motor turns a torque convertor and a clutch hub. The clutch hub is engaged when air pressure is applied to a bladder, forcing the clutch to grab onto the hub. This turns a sprocket gear using a chain in the compound and the compound turns the rotary sprocket once the air rotary handle is engaged by the driller. These air clutches are open when not under pressure from the air. Once the air is applied, the air bladder on the clutch closes grabbing onto a clutch hub. This forces the clutch to turn, therefore forcing the sprocket that is in line with it to turn as well. A diesel electric works a little differently, instead of air clutches; they will have an electric motor that is connected to the gears.

After the kelly and swivel are installed, you can connect any other equipment such as a kelly spinner or iron roughneck. The kelly spinner is an air driven component used to spin the kelly, making a connection or breaking a connection, instead of using the spinning chain. This and the iron roughneck replace the spinning chain in most cases, and allow the driller to avoid placing the rotary table in other gears to perform the same task. The kelly spinner is generally driven by an air gear; it uses an air starter, which when engaged is forced to extend a bendix. The bendix lines up with a flywheel and will then turn the kelly spinner. As the kelly spinner is turned, it works like an impact wrench. When the kelly is placed into another joint of pipe or drill collar, the kelly spinner is engaged, it will be forced to turn, causing the kelly to screw into it, or out of it, as both will have threads to make up to one another. The threads on tubulars are different sometimes and require a crossover sub, or XO sub. Example: some tubulars have XH, FH or IF threads. These types of threads are defined by the weight and strength of the pipe and the connection which they are designed.

There will also be many other things that will need to be installed and rigged up. Most rigs, this day and time have a drilling computer and there are several sensors that will have to be connected. This will need to be done as well, either by the tech or the roughnecks, if they are trained to do so. Remember, there are many different types of rigs; from air rigs to forty thousand feet triples. Communicate with your supervisors and colleagues to ask questions. Learn your rig and your responsibilities when it comes to rigging it up as safely and efficiently as possible. Once you think you are done and can't think of anything else that needs to be done, get with your supervisor and ask what more needs to be rigged up. If your rig has different components that have not been mentioned, you will learn to rig them up and where their proper places are. This book only gives a general Idea of the equipment, the equipment will vary from rig to rig and sometimes things are added or taken away from the rig components. This is where active learning comes into play. As the industry evolves, so must we.

CHAPTER 2

PRE-SPUD INSPECTION

All Inspections are done for the same reason; they are designed to help look for issues or safety infractions that are unsafe. You will not find a problem or potential problem if you're not looking. In this chapter, you'll learn some of the major things that you will have to Inspect. There is of course rig specific things that you may have to inspect that aren't mentioned here. But this will give you an idea of some of the things that you'll need to inspect.

One of the first things that you will have to inspect, are the pins as you install them. The pin inspection will include pins in the derrick, the pins in the derrick shoes, substructure, and the pins in the out-riggers, pipe racks and pits; along with the safety keepers for the pins. All of these pins either have a safety pin that will accompany it, or a bolt to secure it and prevent it from becoming dislodged. This will depend on the position of the pin. For example; if the pin is in the derrick and overhead, a regular bolt wouldn't be satisfactory. If it is in the substructure at foot level, it may work just fine, depending on your company's policy. The rules say that all pins must be secured, but anything overhead, must have a safety bolt with a keeper or safety pin to prevent it from falling onto a worker. If you do find a pin missing a safety keeper, report it to your supervisor, or if you know what is required, you can make the correction and then notify your supervisor.

The next thing that you are going to inspect will more than likely be the grounding rods, cables and clamps. Every piece of equipment that has electricity going to it, or coming from it, must be grounded. This includes anything that has even one light on it. The O.S.H.A. rule states that any and all rig equipment must be grounded if it has electricity going to it, produces electricity or could conduct electricity must be grounded. This will be obtained through a grounding rod connected to the earth and an approved cable that connects the equipment to the rod.

A ground rod will be driven into the ground approximately 4 feet. A specific grounding cable is then attached to the equipment. A potential electrical short is them sent to the ground via a grounding cable, usually double aught (00) cables or solid copper cable, large enough in diameter to safely hold the charge until it is released into the earth.

The ground cable will be connected using a brass clamp at either end connecting the equipment to the earth. If you have any question about the grounding rules, ask your supervisor, as they should know where everything is supposed to be.

The next thing that will be inspected is the electrical wiring on the entire rig; this can usually be inspected visually. You should never grab a wire without inspecting it first. This inspection should be done when the electrical wires were plugged in; it should also be inspected prior to spud. All electrical wiring should be inspected and certified to carry the current for the equipment it is connected to. Basically, you will have an electrical line going to every building. On every piece of equipment which houses a light fixture and other equipment that needs electricity to operate.

The next thing that will be inspected is the safety aspect of the job. O.S.H.A. mandates a lot about the oilfield and is relative to the general construction industry. For example, every hose or line with pressure on it must be secured with a whip-check or safety cable. A whip-check is a flexible cable with two endless loops in it. It is designed with a spring loaded choker assembly and it is used to securely hold a line in the event of a rupture. Other things include a hobble or safety cable bolted to a high pressure line such as the mentioned vibrating hose. These hoses can have more than 5,000 psi on them at any given time, depending on their pressure rating. So it is very important to insure that they cannot flail around and hit someone in the event that they rupture.

The next thing to be inspected is fire extinguishers and housekeeping. OSHA rules state that a fire extinguisher must be placed at any set of stairs leading to the rig floor and on any piece of equipment that houses flammable liquids. These fire extinguishers must be approved for the type of fire that it will be used to extinguish. For example; you cannot use an extinguisher designed to extinguish a chemical fire with a class-A fire extinguisher. It must be compatible with the circumstance and designed to put out a certain type of fire. Most companies use an ABC extinguisher to remove any doubt of its ability to extinguish the fire. The fire extinguishers must be inspected and tagged regularly, as well as filled or replaced if they are not charged properly.

Housekeeping is as big a safety concern as it is a direct reflection of a person's attitude. If your location is kept neat and free from all unnecessary obstructions, then it will be safer and you will be showing everyone, you care about your job and environment. It is also important to remove trip hazards in the event that you need to run away from the area in an emergency situation. The last thing you want is to trip over something if you're running away from a fire or some other emergency. People think that housekeeping is just keeping the trash picked up, but it is a very big safety concern as well. Housekeeping is the general cleanliness of an area. This will include having tools picked up, straightening up after a job and scrubbing the miscellaneous components of the rig that need it. The cleaner you keep your rig and work area, the better you represent yourself and your company's name.

Next you will need to inspect the mud pumps, mud pits and generator/ SCR house. This will include, but is not limited to grounding, electrical, signs, safety guards and hoses being secured properly. You can usually walk around a piece of equipment and see all of these things.

The mud pumps will need to be operated to check their readiness to drill. They can be circulated through the mud pits to check them as well. A pop-off line is used to capture all fluids that come from the mud pump in the event that the pressure relief valve has failed. If the safety pin is removed, you are then able to pump through the pop-off line and ensure that the pump is functioning properly. Any alternate equipment that you have on your rig should also be operated, if possible to make sure it is operational. There are also several forms of paperwork that must be posted in designated areas before any drilling activity can be performed, i.e. drilling permit, plat and inspections performed.

The timeliness that the rig goes on day-work depends upon the readiness of the rig to operate. This of course does not apply to footage rigs. On day rate rigs, the operators are also involved in this inspection process, as oil & gas companies will not accept the rig until all of these things are done and the rig is ready to operate. It is important to have the rig accepted and placed onto day rate, because until it is, it is a financial burden to the drilling contractor.

CHAPTER 3

SPUDDING IN

After you have completed your pre-spud Inspection and made all of the corrections; you will need to get the BHA (Bottom-hole assembly) drill collars on the pipe rack and tally them. Tally is a term which refers to measuring and logging the measurement into a tally book, or on a tally sheet and into the drilling computer if applicable. Remember; do not include the threads in the measurements as they will not be part of the string measurement. The threads will be buried when the tubular is connected, so they are not part of the measurement. Always exclude the threads when using the tally tape. Place the tape on the shoulder of the pin end and then pull your measurement to the end of the box.

After you have your tally, the company man or tool pusher will let you know which bit will be ran. This bit will more than likely be a 12 ¼" or 17" tri-cone drill bit; unless your hole has been pre-drilled and surface casing has already been set. If the well is to be drilled on air, the bit will more than likely be a hammer bit attached to an air hammer. In some cases a much larger bit will be run, depending upon the size of the casing you'll be setting. It is also possible to drill with a tri-cone bit when using air.

These bits called tri-cone will roll around on the bottom of the hole and will allow a lot of weight to be forced onto it. This along with the rotation of the drill string will force the bit to make progress. The weight and RPM's (rotations per minute) together will help the bit cut hole very rapidly.

You may be running an air hammer bit assembly. These bits drill using a pneumatic pressure to actuate a hammer, not unlike a jackhammer. The idea is to only run enough weight to make the hammer hit. Too much weight will shank the hammer and you may be fishing for it. Not enough weight and the hammer will not hit properly and you'll end up with a hard crested bit and similar results.

In either BHA, you will probably be running a bit sub. This attaches to the bottom of a drill-collar and then the bit will be screwed into it. Drill collars are larger and much heavier than regular drill pipe; they are used for their weight and durability. Most wells are spudded in using drill collars in their BHA, but in some cases, the bit is connected directly to the drill pipe, using a bit sub.

After the BHA (bottom hole assembly) is made up, the work is pretty repetitive; you will need to place a drill collar in the mouse hole. (**Mouse hole;** is a stationary hole to store the next tubular to be placed in the drill string. It is also used in the breakdown of the bottom hole assembly or tools). You will then make up the drill collar or tubular onto the kelly or top drive. This will then be placed into the drill string to add weight and length. Weight is used to force the bit to go deeper and helps keep the well-bore straight. The same steps are taken after you have used all of the drill collars that the operator or tool pusher has requested. If using drill collars, and you run all of them, you will be using drill pipe. This process is the same as the drill collars, but it is much easier and quicker than making a connection with drill collars.

The driller will continue to drill the hole to the desired depth (also known as T.D.) as long as you have drill collars and/or drill pipe, or any other tubular required ready for him to use.

CHAPTER 4

DRILLING SURFACE

Never assume that you haven't made a mistake, be cautious and pay attention. You should always double check your work, just as you would check someone else's work if they performed it before you. On most trips, you will not have to strap (measure) out of the hole; but anytime you're tripping to run casing, or you have reached the K.O.P. (Kick off Point) or TD (total depth) you will need to insure that the proper depth has been reached. This is very critical because of the pipe lengths that are needed to case the hole must be accurate.

As the drilling continues, you will need more pipe, we have already covered tallying, and placement of the tubular into the mouse hole. When you place a tubular into the mouse hole, insure that the numbers are visible to the driller. He will need to check it off on his tally sheet that you have given him. Always pick up the tubulars in the same order that you have tallied them. If you pick one up out of order, you could cause confusion in the tally and make the hole depth wrong if a joint were to be removed later.

Now that you are drilling, you will need to finish some tasks not always assigned to someone; these tasks will include straightening up any equipment and/or supplies that were tossed around during the rig move. Almost always you will have to pick up tools and supplies after someone else has left them behind. You will complain and feel taken advantage of, this is why you should always pick your tools and put them in their proper place after a job has been completed.

You will probably need to clean the drainage ditches out daily, as there will be a lot of fluids moving through them. This is all to be done while the drilling operation continues; remember, the well is the reason you are there in the first place.

When the driller knows what the total depth of casing point (TD) of surface hole is going to be, he will then let you know how many joints are estimated to complete the hole. You should have enough drill collars and/or drill pipe on the rack so that he can finish; this will give you a goal. Once you have reached the desired T.D. you will probably have to circulate the hole clean using a sweep (**Sweep;** a chemically comprised recipe of different components used to thicken or increase weight that will help carry the cuttings out of the hole.) This will only take a little time to mix and pump, as most surface casing is set at a depth between 200' and 2,000'.

After you have reached TD and you are circulating, you can be preparing for the trip out. You will need to have your tong dies are in good shape and insure that your tongs and slips are not damaged. (**tong dies;** a hard metal designed to grab onto the pipe without destroying it) (**Slips;** a beveled wedge that have an opening on one side; designed to hold the pipe using its own weight, wedging against the rotary table.) You should already have a bucket of pipe dope on the Rig floor; make sure that you have enough in it to complete the trip. (**Pipe dope;** a chemical compound designed to prevent rust and to provide a semi solid cushion between the treads, this will prevent chatter of the threads and will help the pipe last longer.) Once you begin the trip, you will have to place the stands in a specific order as you rack them on the floor, to allow the derrick man to store them and retrieve them properly. (**Trip;** to pull the drill string out of the hole or place it back into the hole) (**Stand;** a collection of drill pipe or drill collars stacked in order to save time instead of breaking every connection.) These stands are placed on the wooden racking boards made into the rig floor; you will almost always begin racking them on the pit side of the floor, and working your way to the center.

You should rack them all in a symmetrical straight line; this will save room on the floor and will also help you keep a good count of how many stands are out of the hole. You should always number your stands coming out of the hole as well as going in the hole.

Once you have reached the bit, you should cover the hole and then get the bit cleaned up so none of the cuttings fall back down the hole, as this could cause a bridge and make it difficult to pass further down the hole with the casing. Once you have cleaned the bit, you can place the bit breaker in the rotary table and break the bit. Remember, the breakout tongs go on top of the break, except above the kelly, everything below the kelly is right handed threads; everything above the kelly, is left handed threads. As your tripping out of the hole, the breakout tongs should always go on top; the makeup tongs should be on the bottom of the break.

Now you're ready to rig up the casing crew to run casing. This will usually include a power tong operator, a stabber and two floor hands. First, you'll need to attend a safety meeting to discuss any issues or instances that could cause bodily injury. A pre-job safety meeting with everyone who will be involved in the operation, should prevent any confusion and will also help everyone know what the next step will be. After the safety meeting, you'll more than likely help pull the hydraulic hoses up to the rig floor. Then, you'll need to use the air tugger or cat-line to bring up the power tongs, slips, & other miscellaneous equipment needed to run the casing.

CHAPTER 5

RUNNING SURFACE CASING

We will begin picking up one joint of casing (Usually 9 5/8" 32# j-55 LT&C casing for surface) the first joint is called the shoe joint. We will make up the float collar and down jetted guide, float shoe or Texas shoe onto it. (Sometimes the shoe will be tack welded or strap welded onto the shoe joint to prevent slipping.) Insure that you have changed the tong head to the proper size so they will fit the casing. This OD (outside diameter) will be larger than the drill pipe and drill collars that you've just tripped out of the hole. After you pick up the shoe joint, you will usually apply a thread lock compound to the threads which will insure that the shoe will be cemented in place onto the first joint of casing. This compound has an industry nickname called thread cement. Once the thread lock compound has been applied, the tong operator will torque the casing to the recommended torque. He will set his needle on the torque gauge to the recommended torque and will make all connections up to this torque. This process will continue until TD has been reached with the casing.

After all surface casing has been run into the well-bore; you must break circulation and circulate while you rig the casing crew down. This procedure is a normal policy and is in place; in the event that the casing has become plugged or circulation is not allowed for any other reason, all of the casing would have to be pulled out of the well-bore using the power tongs. So don't rig them down before you break circulation. Once you have established circulation, you can rig down the casing crew and release them from the rig site.

You should have cementers on location by now. After you have had a safety meeting, you're ready to rig them up and you can begin pulling their equipment up onto the floor using an air tugger or cat-line. The equipment used in the cementing job will include a cementing head, cementing beals, and high pressure hoses or steel lines.

A safety meeting will be held to make sure both companies' policies and procedures are followed prior to beginning the job. This is always a good practice because you will find out the process and avoid confusion on anyone's part. During the cementing operation there will be a lot of activity. Your supervisor will let you know where you should be and your responsibilities. (Warning: never step over a line, always assume that a line has pressure on it! If it is required that you be around pressurized lines, walk around them if possible, or step on top of them, do not step on a connection. If a sudden release of pressure were to occur, the line would flail around and could cause serious injury or even death. The best practice is to step on a pressurized line. In the event of a sudden release of pressure, you would be lifted up, instead of cut in half.)

It is a must to maintain circulation throughout the cementing job. If you notice that you have lost returns, notify your supervisor right away. If you see that a line has started leaking, notify your supervisor. Never hit a line under pressure to tighten it up. Hitting a line under pressure could cause it to explode and can kill. If returns are lost, a squeeze or grouting job may be necessary. Grouting casing is simple, you simply place a 1" cementing joint down the back side of the casing and pump cement until it reaches the surface. Squeezing cement is similar and can be done fairly easy as well. Once the cementers are done, you will assist them in rigging down. A waiting period of four to eight hours is usually required on the surface cement before the casing can be used.

CHAPTER 6

BLOWOUT PREVENTERS

(**Blowout Preventer;** a mechanically or hydraulically operated piece of equipment used in the event of a pressure release down hole.)

A blowout preventer (B.O.P.) is a mandatory piece of equipment that will prevent any escaping gasses from entering the atmosphere. This will be done by containing the gases and/or diverting them to a designated place. This piece of equipment is a lifesaver. All B.O.P.'s are certified from the factory and must be tested periodically to insure their integrity is in compliance.

There are two different types of preventers; the ram type preventer and the bladder type preventer. The ram type preventer is a screw type preventer. To activate this type of preventer, a screw must be turned on either side of the body, thus forcing the ram to press against the tubular and prevents any fluid or well-bore material from escaping around the annulus of the pipe. These screws are turned by a hydraulic ram. In the event that these hydraulic rams fail, a manual handle can be placed onto the screw and turned manually to close the rams, resulting in the same effect.

The annular or bladder type preventer is a stationary type of preventer that uses fluid to inflate a bladder and works similar to the ram type preventer. The annular preventer seals off around the tubular to prevent all well-bore fluids from escaping. This is only a fluid forced bladder and cannot be manually closed.

These types of preventers are rated for the pressures that they can restrict or hold back from the well-bore. For example; a 5,000lb preventer can prevent 5,000lbs of force from the well-bore. A 3,000lb preventer can restrict 3,000lbs of force on the well-bore. These are also available in 10,000lb and 15,000lb preventers.

All preventers and other well control equipment must be tested every 27 days, or as your company or operator requires. Some operators require an inspection and pressure test every 21 days; this will be mandated by the operator and the areas that you are working in.

A BOP and all of the BOPE (blow out preventer equipment) is used to keep you and the environment safe from the sudden release of volatile fluids, gas or a combination of both from escaping. The sudden release of these gases or fluids can cause an ignition immediately and could kill everyone on site and burn the rig down.

All states have oil & gas Inspectors and they will insure that the inspections are documented and available for anyone to see. The BOP includes every component from the wellhead to the last preventer. There are also kill line valves, manual closing valves and HCR (hydraulic choke ram) valves. These valves are for a specific reason and should be inspected and maintained for safety. The kill line valve serves as an avenue to pump fluids into the annulus (outside of the pipe) of the well to kill it in case of an emergency. The kill valve allows the kill mud which is weighted heavy enough to suppress the influx. The HCR is in the other side of the mud cross and is an outlet of the well fluids in the event of a release. The annular or pipe rams would be closed and the fluids will be sent through the choke line manual valve and then to the HCR valve (some rigs do not have HCR valves) and then to the choke.

The choke is a manifold of different valves and chokes which allow you to control how much pressure you release at any given time. The choke manifold then expels the fluid or gas to the gas buster or a panic line. The panic line will then either send the fluid or gas to the reserve pit or a flare stack or flare tank. The flare tank or flare stack is where the excess gas from the gas buster will be ignited at a safe distance from the rig and personnel and burned off until it is under control.

The gas buster also separates the fluid from the gas and reclaims the fluid into the active mud pits. Each one of these components serves a vital purpose and should be treated as a safety tool which may save your life one day.

CHAPTER 7

NIPPLE UP B.O.P.'S

Now that you have cemented the surface casing and it has set for the curing time, you're ready to nipple up the B.O.P.'s (also called a stack)

The first thing that will need to be done is to dress the casing and install the wellhead. This is the base of the stack as it is welded or screwed onto the casing that we have previously cemented into the ground. A welder will be on location if needed and will weld on the wellhead. This is a tedious job for the welder, as the wellhead must be square, level and the wellhead must be certified to hold the specified pressures. First the welder will dress the casing using a cutting torch and a grinder. It will need to be symmetrical and have almost a factory cut to support the wellhead. After the casing is dressed, the welder will have the wellhead placed onto the casing. He will then align the wellhead to the desired position and begin a root pass, which will connect the two materials. Then he will make a hot pass, which will fill in most of the gap remaining from the factory bevel for welding. This will tie the wellhead and casing together by making several passes; this will insure that there is a good seal. The final weld that is made will be the cap pass. The cap is made using a large fast burning rod.

Once the welder is finished welding, the wellhead must cool to within acceptable testing temperatures. Then the welder will test the wellhead to the allotted pressure to certify its capability. After the wellhead has been tested & documented as a pass, you can begin the nipple up process. Usually, you will have your bolts cleaned & ready to be installed. Now you can lift the stack and place it onto the wellhead using a pick up line.

This is a line usually 1" which has sufficient capability to lift the BOP. This line will go through the hook on the blocks and then down to the stack on either side of the rotary table. You will connect one line to one side of the stack and the other side using the other line. Remember, you must go in opposite directions as you bridle the lines onto the stack. This will prevent the stack from turning as it is raised and lowered. In some instances, you will use hoists or heavy lift wenches to lift your stack and set it in place; this is much safer than with a pick up line. (Don't forget the compression ring also known as an API ring) if you don't place the compression ring in properly, the stack will leak and you will have to repeat a lot of your work. Once you begin to lift the stack onto the wellhead, you will need to be careful about being under a suspended load. You must put bolts in all of the holes and tighten them using a hammer wrench or in some cases, an impact wrench.

After you have all of the bolts tight, you can remove the bridle lines from the stack, or rig down the hoist or wenches. You can now finish the nipple up process. (Some stacks will stay together; this means that the annular will not be removed from the ram preventers.) However in some cases you will need to place the annular on top of the ram preventer; this also uses studs and nuts to secure the annular to the ram preventer. The nuts and bolts will need to be tightened before you can remove the bridle line. Now comes the tedious part, you need to connect the hydraulic lines to their proper place. There are two lines for every ram preventer and every annular preventer. You will have one line that will open the valve & one that will close the valve. This means that you will have to investigate the lines and the preventer in order to have the right placement. After you have them all hooked up, the preventers should be function tested to insure all valves work properly.

Now you can hook up the manual kill line valve and the HCR (hydraulic choke ram) valve. This will require a hydraulic line to open it and one to close it. After this is complete, you can hook up the choke line and choke manifold, which will have a large 4" line from the HCR valve to the choke manifold. This will receive fluid or gas from the stack and will allow you to hold back the pressure so it can be controlled in the event that you are receiving high pressures.

Now you must hook up the choke manifold, (**choke manifold;** a pre configured set of valves and chokes set in a line to assist in the restriction of fluids or gas migrating to the surface.) After your choke manifold is connected and tight, you can hook up your gas buster and panic line. (**Panic line;** a 2" or 4" line used to divert fluids and gases to their proper place usually sent to the reserve pit or a flare stack.) You will also have two 6" or 8" lines that will carry the fluid to the possum belly of your shaker from the gas buster. These lines allow you to retrieve fluids as they are separated from the gas migration.

CHAPTER 8

TESTING THE B.O.P.'S

All components that may have pressure on them must be tested to their certified pressure. A certified tester will be on location to test all of the prevention equipment and certify each component. Remember, as the lines pressure up, there could be 250# to the maximum capacity of your stack, up to 15,000# on these lines. **(STAY AWAY!)** If the tester has a leak, let him know. (Never touch a line with pressure on it and always assume there is pressure.) If there is a leak, after you are sure that all of the pressures are relieved and it is safe; you will need to tighten the flange or replace the faulty piece of equipment and then it must be re-tested until it passes.

This is a required test and an OSHA mandated certification as well. The industry standard is 70% of the annular's pressure capability and 100% of the ram preventer's capability. (The test that is more commonly performed is called a low/hi test.) Most annular preventers are lower pressure than their sister ram component.

There can be several combinations of stacks used in different configurations to obtain the pressure capability desired. (Example; there may be four ram preventers and two annular preventers.) As the tester tests each component, he will let the driller know if there are any components that will need to be corrected and/or replaced.

In the event that you need to replace a component, you will need to replace the compression ring for that component as well; the failure usually starts with the compression ring. Now that the stack and all the other equipment have been tested and are certified to pass, you can begin picking up the next BHA and get ready for the drillout from surface casing.

CHAPTER 9

DRILLOUT

(**DRILLOUT**; is a term used to describe Drilling out from under surface or intermediate casings to begin drilling new formation.)

You will be picking up a new drill bit, bit sub, and a total new BHA; but this may include some of the BHA that was used to drill the surface hole. You will more than likely still be using the drill collars. You will have several different types of BHA's this will change depending upon the area you are drilling in and what types of formation you are going to be going through.

The different types of formations that you can go through will depend on the area of the world you are drilling in. For instance, in west Texas, you will be drilling through clays, anti-hydrate, chert, lime, chalk and lots of different types of shale's. Some shale's will be gas producing and some shale's will be oil producers and others a sour gas producer, depending upon the formation's periods of formation and the pressures at those depths. The properties of these shale's are a timeline of history in which billions and even trillions of plants, biological multi cell life, and single cell organisms died and began the decomposition stage. This combined with many landslides and lower settlement formations are what produces the shale's that we all search so desperately to find and produce. The decomposing matter began to produce a multitude of different gases as the years passed and now we are producing so many of these gases for use in major production factories, heating our homes, energy production and even to pressurize other formations to store other chemicals.

The gases that we are interested in producing are methane, ethane, butane and other safe flammable natural gas. (There are other formations other than shale which produce oil, coal and natural gas. In most areas where coal is found, you will also find (CBM) coal bed methane. This is an optimum heating Gas, but it was too difficult to mass produce until the late 1980's. Now there are three times as many coal bed methane wells producing in the Unites States as there are shale gas wells. The reason for this, the zones are shallow and that makes it easier to pinpoint the production zones.)

Now that we are ready to trip in the hole with our new BHA; you'll make up the bit and torque it. You will more than likely run the entire length of pipe in the derrick into the hole. Once you have reached the desired depth, you will have to perform a casing pressure test. (**CPT**) a casing pressure test is designed to test the integrity of the casing shoe. It is not a requirement for all states in the U.S. however, in the states that this test is required; it must be performed before the drillout can continue. To perform the casing pressure test you will have the pumps clutch off and close the annular preventer. (Only close the annular if there is no pressure on the drill pipe.) Once the annular preventer has been closed, you can begin pressuring up on the casing. There are two ways to do this; your driller will engage the pump clutches in and out until the desired pressure is on the casing shoe. The second method is to use a mobile hydraulic pump to pump water or mud down the casing to pressure up on it. This tests the casing shoe because the shoe is the weakest point of the casing. 1,500psi for 15 minutes will more than likely be the test parameters that are required, but could change with the operator or contractor.

After the casing pressure test has been conducted and documented, you are ready to begin drilling cement. The cement that you will be drilling is the same cement that we used to cement the surface casing. There will be some cement on top of the plug that is wedged into the port on the casing shoe. This cement will need to be drilled out before we are able to proceed. After the cement has been drilled, the shoe will be next and this may take up to two hours to drill through.

Once you have drilled through the shoe, you will continue drilling cement for a while, then, there will be more than likely be a void under the cement into the formation. The void will that you will encounter will be the change in formation, from cement to the new hole. In some cases, there is one other test you will be performing; this test is a F.I.T. Test. (Formation Integrity Test) this test checks the formation below the shoe for the amount of pressure that it would allow before it would breakdown and fail. This means, that the formation at a specific pressure would break down at that section of the well-bore; this is more than likely the loss zone that would be encountered and you would begin losing fluid into the formation.

This test is conducted by the driller as well. The driller will turn off the pump and let all pressures bleed off. Then he will close the annular preventer and begin putting pressure onto the formation. This pressure is always determined by the geologist and the drilling engineers as they calculate the ECD (equivalent circulating density) at this point. Now that you have performed all tests necessary, you can continue drilling ahead.

CHAPTER 10

VERTICAL WELLS

(**Vertical;** to describe a position in a straight up and down line, in an upright position, or running lengthwise up or down)

A vertical well is somewhat self explanatory. This well will continue straight down from surface to T.D. It will be handled in a very conventional way. There will be several ways to drill this well, but the end desirable result will be a perfectly straight hole. These wells will more than likely be oil wells or shallow gas wells and in some cases deeper gas baring formation wells that are not feasible for horizontal production. The oil wells need to be straight to prevent any rubbing on the casing by the rods or swab assembly. After a well is perforated, it will be fraced and sometimes even acidized to optimize production. These assemblies use a submersible pump that will pull fluid up the hole on the up stroke, this process will be repeated until fluid is forced out of the hole. The gas wells, coal bed methane, or other vertical gas wells use a compressed gas lift and require no other assistance. The gas wells only need to be perforated and fraced to allow the gasses to escape from its resting place.

All over the world, in every country, wherever you see a pump jack, there is a straight hole with this type of assembly being used to pull oil out of the ground. Gas wells use either a lift station or injection assistance method. The gas well is usually only recognizable by a series of pipe and gauges on top the ground where the well was drilled. In some cases, a compressor station or some other type of gas specific equipment will be showing. The vertical oil wells are more distinguishable by the iconic pump jack.

CHAPTER 11

HORIZONTAL WELLS

(**Horizontal well;** a well that is drilled from a vertical point and then using a method of directional drilling, it will be placed horizontal and then drilled to T.D.)

A horizontal well is used primarily for gas only. They are designed to gain an optimum amount of vertical section in a specific pay zone. This is a very prolific design, as it optimizes the area of a gas producing shale's performance and makes it easier for us to produce. Once you have drilled the well and ran casing, the completion crew will come in and perforate and frac these types of wells. This will allow the gas to migrate into the well-bore and flow up to the production head with massive amounts of pressure.

These natural gas wells don't usually play out as fast as the oil wells do because they are not forced to produce; thus, the formation pressures keep these types of wells producing for years. There is however other ways to force these gas wells to produce faster than they normally would. Some operators choose to use injection as a way to help the gas baring formation stay pressurized. Some operators inject carbon dioxide, carbon monoxide, and other expendable air gases to help pressurize the gas baring formations.

CHAPTER 12

DIRECTIONAL WELLS

(**Directional well;** a well that is drilled from a vertical point and then using a mud motor and MWD for directional steering, it will be turned to a certain direction. After the angle of deflection has been obtained and the well-path is planned it will be placed in that azimuth and inclination, then Drilled to T.D.)

A directional well is usually a perfect application to avoid another close proximity well. The direction can be changed using a tangent to alter the direction and stay away from the other well to avoid an underground collision. A directional well is not only a horizontal well, but may have several turns and tangents designed into it. The reason to take a well-bore in a certain direction is to avoid certain fractures that are known to geologist and drilling engineers who plan the well-path. In some extreme cases, these wells will obtain a massive negative vertical section (behind the vertical line) to avoid a collision or fault.

Once you have drilled the well and ran casing, the completion crew will come in and perforate and then frac these type of wells. This will allow the gas to migrate into the well-bore and flow up to the production head.

The same concept applies to directional wells as to the horizontal wells. These wells don't usually play out as fast as the oil wells do, because they are not forced to produce and thus, the formation pressures keep these types of wells producing for years. Some directional wells are then drilled horizontally and some go back to vertical after the tangent has been placed into the well-bore

Chapter 13

Total Depth (TD)

(**TD;** total depth of a well has been reached, or a stage of the well has been completed.)

T.D. is a term that defines different stages of the well, as we've said before; there are several different stages of a well. You will have a T.D. for surface, for Intermediate, if you're running Intermediate casing, there will be a T.D. for a Curve and for the final total depth of a well where you will run production casing. Or in some extreme instances, you will P & A the Well. (**P&A;** plug & abandon a well, if the well turns out to be a dry hole, or too troublesome to produce.) There is always a T.D. on a well; no matter the circumstances and no matter the final outcome, there will always be a T.D. even a well that ultimately is a P&A, there is still a TD that is reported to the railroad commission, DEP (Department of Environmental Protection) or BLM (Bureau of Land Management.)

At T.D. there will be several things that are happening. There will be times that you will circulate several times the hole's capacity. You will be sweeping the hole & pumping pills to clean the cuttings out and bring them to surface. There can be several ways of cleaning the hole and keeping it in its most optimum shape for running casing. If you are at a stage T.D.

then you are treating it for the next stage of tripping and running casing.

CHAPTER 14

TRIPPING PIPE

(**Tripping Pipe;** to pull the string out of the hole or putting it back into the hole.)

As we trip pipe, it is different on each rig; some rigs are single lay downs, and some are doubles and pull two joints of pipe each time, that defines the number of joints that are left together in a stand. Stands get their name from leaning the pipe in the derrick and standing them upright. Another example is triples, which leave three joints of pipe together in a stand. There are also single rack back rigs. These are four different types of rigs that are the most typical and most often used.

During the tripping operation, there are certain steps that will be repeated until the job is completed. The object of tripping pipe is to retrieve or change out something in the string or even the BHA. It could be to find a hole in the drill pipe or drill collars detected by a loss of pressure; or to simply wipe the hole clean to remove any hole problems.

Sometimes it is necessary to change the BHA several different times during a well. For example; if you're drilling a directional well and you need 14° degree doglegs to hit your target and you're only getting 8° degrees or 9°degrees per hundred; it would be a necessity to trip and change the bend in the motor to insure that you receive the doglegs that you need, rather than fight it and land lower than your planned target. (**Doglegs;** a calculation of build rates at which your well-bore is building.)

Another instance when it is in your best interest to trip is; your P-Rate is not satisfactory and you could do better with a different bit, then you would trip and change your bit. (**Penetration Rate;** the rate measured in footage or time, at which you penetrate the earth with the drill string.) This is much easier than fighting the P-Rate and needing to drill the hole faster but not having the performance of a sharp bit. A sharper bit, better hole cleaning and a number of other parameters mediate the rate at which the drill string will penetrate the formations. These also mandate at which point you trip to change a drilling assembly to optimize your performance.

CHAPTER 15

LAYING DOWN DRILL PIPE

Laying down drill pipe & drill collars is an operation that is performed at the end of the well or a when a change in drill pipe size is required. When you pull the entire drill string out of the hole, or just part of it and Lay it down; including drill pipe and drill collars. You will usually lay down the pipe before you run production casing; because you cannot trip the pipe into the hole after you have the casing production ran, due to the ID (inside diameter of the casing. In some cases, you will run the production casing prior to laying the drill pipe down; this is usually mandated by an emergency hole conditions and a time sensitive situation.

There are a couple of ways that drill pipe is laid down. If your rig is not equipped with a lay down arm, one operational technique is to use a lay down machine. This is a machine that uses a long half open piece of larger diameter pipe to receive the drill pipe or drill collars, then lower it to the catwalk and dump it out. Then you can remove the pipe from the pipe rack and place it in its proper place.

This could be a very long process as each joint of range II pipe averages 31.50' and range III pipe averages 44.5'. If you're running range II pipe and your well is 10,000' deep then you would have to lay down 317 joints minus your BHA; so if you are laying down a joint every three minutes then it would take you approximately 15 ¾ hours.

That's a lot of time performing the same daunting operation; so if you must do it, try not to be complacent. Complacency is the mother of all incidents. Being complacent is a state of mind that a person gets into

when they become comfortable with their surroundings and do not expect them to change, so try and keep focused. Remember what you're doing and where you're hand and foot placement should be. Remember that if you place your hands somewhere that they shouldn't be, then you may lose them.

As the driller pulls the pipe up through the rotary table then you should have the slips ready to be set. After your slips are set, depending on which side of the pipe you're working on, your tongs will go in different places. If you're on the off driller's side, your tongs will be placed on the top joint; these are the break-out tongs. If you're working on the driller's side, your tongs will be placed on the lower joint, these are the make-up tongs. After the tongs are on, the driller will begin pulling on the tongs and break the connection.

Once the connection is broke, then you will either have a set of pipe spinners, an iron roughneck, or the driller will use the rotary table to rotate out the pipe. Once the pipe is free, the driller will raise it out of the stump and then it can be placed into the trough and then lowered to the floor. After it is lowered to the floor then it can be unlatched and released from the elevators so the operator of the lay down machine can lower it down and it can be released onto the pipe rack. We will continue this process until the entire string of pipe is laid down.

CHAPTER 16

RUNNING INTERMEDIATE CASING

Running Intermediate casing is the same as running any other casing, except for it will hang off of a set of casing slips inside of the wellhead or on the bottom of the surface casing, via a casing hanger. This process is called hanging casing. This technique is more reasonable to most operators because you do not have to nipple down the stack to set the casing in most cases.

Intermediate casing is set because the operator wants to protect a specific zone from contamination; or it can also be used to prevent problems that a certain formation may be causing to the well-bore. These formations, such as wetting shale, or a temperature sensitive formation can be problematic. Formations such as these can cause lots of problems; because the further down you drill into earth, the formations are less and less compatible. Some formations need for us to maintain a certain water loss with our mud properties. (**Water loss;** is the rate at which the water of the drilling fluid is lost into the formation, allowing the formation to become wet and swell from contamination.) If you continue to drill at an optimum water loss for one formation; another formation may be sensitive and you could cause that problematic formation to cavitate or swell; this could ruin the entire well-bore over a small section.

The other reasons to run intermediate casing may be to have the option to produce that formation later or to protect the formation from the drilling activity, such as contaminating a deep water stream. The operator may have cemented the original formation that they were producing. This

is an option for formations that may now be depleted. The operator could enter the wall of the intermediate casing and drill a new formation; then perforate a formation further up the hole and produce it as well.

As we drill through formations, we sometimes purposely avoid contaminating them, in hopes that we can come back to them later. In many cases; these formations produce lots of salt water and fresh water that we do not wish to dispose of. (Example; during the normal drilling of an oil well around Odessa, Texas, you drill through the Glorietta formation to get to the pay zone. The Glorietta is an oil baring formation and the operator may later choose to produce this formation for oil; after he has depleted the oil baring formations below in ten or fifteen years.)

We will begin picking up one joint of casing (usually 7" or 8 5/8" LT&C casing.) This is the shoe joint. We will make up the float collar and down jetted guide shoe onto it. (Sometimes the shoe will be tack welded, or strap welded onto the shoe joint to prevent slipping.) After we pick up the shoe joint, we will use a thread lock compound to insure it will be cemented in place.

Once the thread lock compound has been applied, the tong operator will torque it to the recommended torque. He will set his needle on the recommended torque and will make all connections up to the specified torque. You will then run all joints required to reach the intermediate T.D. Centralizers will be placed periodically to center the casing. After all Intermediate casing has been run; you must break circulation and circulate while you're rigging the casing crew down.

CHAPTER 17

RUNNING PRODUCTION CASING

Production casing is the casing that the well will produce the master product (oil or gas) and then send it to the pipeline, the lift station, production plant or to the tank battery on site. This casing will be run all the way to T.D. of the well and will then be cemented into place and later perforated and fraced.

Running production casing is the same as running any other casing, except for it will hang off of a set of casing slips inside of the wellhead. This process is called hanging casing. Often you are able to lower the casing slips through the stack and then set the desired weight onto the slips. When available, this technique is more appeasable because you do not have to nipple down the stack to set the casing. In other cases; you will nipple down the stack and set the casing slips from the bottom. This is so that you are able to seat the slips and insure the weight is optimum.

We will begin by picking up one joint of casing which is the shoe joint, (usually 5 ½" or 4 ½" 17# or 20# LT&C casing.) We will make up the float shoe and float collar onto the first joint of casing. (Sometimes the shoe may be tack welded onto the shoe joint to prevent slipping.) After we pick up the shoe joint, we will use a thread lock compound to insure it will be cemented in place. Once the thread lock compound has been applied, the tong operator will torque it to the recommended torque. He will set his needle on the recommended torque and will make all connections up to the specified torque.

You will then run all joints required to reach T.D. of the well; centralizers

will be placed periodically to center the casing inside of the well-bore. After all production casing has been run, you must break circulation and circulate while you rig the casing crew down and then rig up the cementers. You will cement the production casing to surface in most cases. This will prevent and well-bore fluids or gases from migrating to surface through the well's annulus.

CHAPTER 18

RIG RELEASE

Rig release is an important time of the well. This is the point that the rig goes off of its normal day rate and then begins its mobilization rate, if applicable. This could mean thousands of dollars in revenue lost for every day that the rig isn't on the normal day rate. If the rig doesn't perform at its optimum level then it will lose money, so it is very important to get the rig moved as efficiently as possible. The idea is to get the rig back on the operator's payroll as soon as possible.

Once we have run the production casing and cemented, then we will be ready to rig the cementers down. After the cementers are rigged down, we must do something else; we must clean the pits (mud tanks) before we can begin rigging the other equipment down. We must also nipple down and set the casing slips. Setting the casing slips is a simple job; it will usually be performed by a qualified technician. You will simply nipple down the BOP and the driller will raise it to allow access for the slip hand to set the slips, unless the casing slips are set through the stack. The slips must be set and the tanks must be cleaned, this is always done before a rig is released. You will now to begin rigging the rig equipment down.

CHAPTER 19

RIGGING DOWN

This is the point where you can make rigging up easier by putting things in their proper place and making them accessible for the future rig up on the next well. This means that you will have to plan ahead in anticipation so that it will be easier if you are rigging up what you rigged down. If you plan on rigging up all of the equipment that you rig down, then you would be more likely to have things in order. We will begin rigging down the back yard. The pits come first and then the pumps and other miscellaneous equipment. It should only take a couple of hands to rig down the back yard. The rest of the crew should be on the drill floor rigging it down.

After the back yard is rigged down, then the floor and floor equipment will come next. This will be easier than rigging up the equipment because it is already there. You simply need to place it in its transportation mode. The tongs will probably go in the junk basket as well as the drill subs and floor valves. Most equipment has its own place during every rig move. You will have to ask where everything is supposed to go and then you will know from then on.

After the floor is rigged down, the derrick can be laid over and placed onto the derrick stand. Once this is done, you can un-spool the drilling line and roll it neatly in a pre determined place. This will make everything run smoothly as it is loaded up and moved to the next location.

After the drilling line is placed where it is supposed to be, you can begin rigging down the derrick lines. This will include any tugger lines, airlines, and cables that are hanging from the derrick during normal drilling operations. In most cases, the derrick will have to be separated for the move. This is on the larger rigs and can be ignored on the singles and some doubles.

When you have all of the drilling equipment rigged down and ready to load out, you still have to get all of the non-essential loads ready to be moved as well. These loads are the loads that are not permitted and can be moved even on a weekend. This will include tubulars, suitcases, the airlines and waterlines, etc. Once the rig is ready to be loaded out, you are ready for trucks to mobilize your rig to the next location.

CHAPTER 20

RIG EQUIPMENT

Rig equipment will vary from rig to rig, some rigs will have top drives and some will have a kelly. Some will have an Iron roughneck and some will simply use tongs and/or a kelly spinner, and so on and so forth.

All rigs that are equipped with a top drive will be more likely to be on a well where there is going to be trouble with torque issues or where the well is going to take longer to drill. These wells are all over the world and are more typical, now that we have to go deeper to find the oil and gas to supply our countries demands. In some instances, the operator prefers a top drive rig over a kelly rig simply because of the simplicity of the operation and the ability to back ream. A top drive rig makes a connection every 60' or 90' (excluding a single derrick rigs) depending upon the size of the rig. A kelly rig must make a connection every 30' this is why some operators prefer a top drive over a kelly rig. On average, each connection can take up to 8 minutes, so if you're only making a connection every sixty or ninety feet, then you're saving an average of 16 minutes per stand on a triple and 8 minutes on a double. This could save a lot of time over the course of a 10,000' well.

An iron roughneck is a hydraulic tool used to replace the tongs and kelly spinner as well as the pipe spinners on a trip. This is a very idealistic piece of equipment for this reason. Not only does it replace the need for these other pieces of equipment, but it can be operated by one man instead of two or three men. The iron roughneck is stationary and when activated, it will move toward the pipe, grab onto it, and break it loose or tighten it up; then it will spin the pipe out or spin it into the opposing connection. This is all done at the remote station, which are the operator's controls for the iron roughneck.

An iron roughneck can be set so it will torque the pipe to the recommended torque; this is so the operator doesn't have to focus on the torque as much as he would if the equipment wouldn't stop at a certain torque. This will free the operator up to focus on other things, such as the hand placement of the other employees. As you become more familiar with your equipment, you will be able to make a connection or trip pipe as fast as or faster than the rigs with manual equipment.

A rig equipped with tongs will usually be a power rig; this means that it will use a cable or chain to pull the tongs around and break the connection. Tongs are like giant pipe wrenches that pull hard against the pipe to tighten it or break it apart. They come in different sizes and models. The most common brand is Echo and Wooly Booger made in Odessa, Texas. Some Wooly Booger tongs are still in existence but they are ancient in retrospect to the modern oilfield equipment which will do everything for you. Trust me; I've used both and if you're not familiar with the term "putting out" you'll learn it very quickly by using a 4' set of Wooly Booger tongs. If your rig has tongs, then you will be trained in the proper technique and operation. The idea is to work smarter, not harder. If you use your mind more often, then you won't have to use your back as much. When you learn the correct way to use them and become proficient, you will be hard to beat in their operational performance.

For rigs with a kelly, it is a rotary table that drives this assembly to make the pipe turn. The kelly is a hex pipe or square pipe that has either four or six sides to it. This is placed into a set of rotary bushings and is then is set into a square hole in the rotary table. The rotary table is turned using a drive chain connected to the draw works. This forces the pipe to turn and using weight that you allow to be on the bit, you can drill a hole in the ground.

A top drive rig has another advantage over a kelly rig. This is plain to see while you're drilling. On a top drive, you will use hydraulic power. A hydraulic unit is placed in a strategic place and connected to the top drive. The driller uses the control panel to make the top drive turn; break or make up the connection at the top of the joint, and open or close a lower kelly valve when necessary. This takes the place of the tongs on the upper connection. It also takes the place of the rotary table and another employee when using the manual actuation of the lower kelly valve. This is a time saver on three different levels.

The top drive is also advantageous in a situation where you may need to back ream a stand of pipe out of the hole due to hole problems. With a kelly, you cannot back ream. The kelly can only be turned to the right if it is in gear. This means that the draw works must be in gear also. So if you have a kelly, you can only rotate the pipe if you're going down; you wouldn't be back reaming, you would just simply be reaming. As it is not usually possible to rotate and pick up on the string at the same time with a kelly rig.

Now we move on to the mud pumps. Pumps, or mud pumps, are large mechanically driven fluid pumps that force fluid into one part of the pump, called the fluid end suction. Then the fluid is forced out of the pump in the fluid end discharge; it works like a straw. If you suck on a straw, you are able to pull fluid in and hold it until you are ready to release it.

This is the same thing that a mud pump does. It will hold a vacuum on the fluid that it pulls into it and then release it with a force to push it out of the pump into the standpipe. The fluid then goes through the standpipe to the kelly hose and then down the pipe, all the way to the bit. This is where the fluid, or mud, comes into the drilling of a an oil or gas well. The fluid is a combination of chemicals used as a coolant. It also houses a yield point property which is a point at which a solid is sustained or suspended in the fluid.

The fluid, or mud, is then forced out of the hole, just as if you were filling a glass of water. The more you pour in, the more comes out; so as the fluid is forced out, the drill solids are forced out as well due to the suspension properties of the mud.

Think of it this way; if you're drilling a hole in a piece of wood using a hand drill, you will get wooden shavings as you bore through it. You would have to brush away the shavings, or blow them out of the way; this is called displacement. You are displacing the wood with the drill bit and a hole that is left behind. The longer the drill bit, the more area you will displace. This is the same concept as drilling a hole in the ground.

The farther you drill down, the more materials you are displacing. They have to go somewhere, so we need to get them out of the way before they fall down back onto the drill bit. Just as you would when you drill a hole into wood and the shavings fall into the drilled hole; you are simply doing it on a grander scale. If we continued to drill without cleaning the cuttings out of the way, they would simply fall back down onto the bit. As they fall onto the bit, it would bind up and eventually stop drilling.

There are so many pieces of equipment that are rig specific; we cannot cover all of them. We will discuss, however the most common types of equipment. These are some of the more commonplace types of equipment listed below in alphabetical order.

EQUIPMENT NAMES:

AIR COMPRESSOR; a pneumatic force is created when an engine runs, causing pistons to compress air and build pressure. These are used in air drilling operations and are quite productive.

AIR HAMMER; A pneumatic housing that has a piston and a shaft and compression ring that resembles a jackhammer, when functioning properly. It extends the shaft out of the end of it causing the hammer bit to hit the ground in the well-bore. This combined with the rotation drills the hole.

BEALS; are a long solid tubular hangers that will hold the elevators to the blocks during a trip.

BLOCKS; are a cluster of sheaves that the drilling line runs through to raise and lower the traveling equipment. This is part of the traveling equipment that holds the swivel, Kelly, or top drive and beals with the elevators during different procedures. This equipment is different on all rigs and has many different manufacturers.

BOOSTER; A booster assists in creating more pressure in the line delivering the air volume to the well-bore. This allows the well to be drilled with fewer compressors than it would otherwise take to obtain the same amount of volume.

B.O.P's; is an acronym for blow out preventer's, also called a stack, this is a piece of equipment designed to contain and/or divert any unwanted release of well bore gases that may be released during normal drilling operations.

DERRICK; is a tower structure that is certified to withstand a certain amount of weight. This weight is in a downward force. This is where the pipe is stored during a trip and all of the traveling equipment is housed during normal drilling operations.

DRAW WORKS; is a collection of gears; with multiple gears inside of a gear box, designed to provide a movement not unlike a clock movement once they are engaged. This is where the drilling line is spooled and released during the entirety of the well. This is also what raises and lowers the derrick.

DRILL COLLARS; are extra heavy duty tubulars which can withstand enormous amounts of weight and force. These are usually added to the drill string to provide more weight and cannot be broken as easily as drill pipe.

DRILLING LINE; is a braded wire rope, designed to withstand a lot of weight. This is the muscle of the operation and it is a necessity on any drilling rig. Any rig of any shape or size uses drilling line to move the traveling equipment.

DRILLING MUD; this is the blood of a well. This acts as a coolant and an extractor of drill solids. Without drilling mud, the hole would collapse under the force of the earth and atmospheric pressures down hole. Certain weights and pressure gradients are a necessity at different depths of every well. This is engineered by a trained professional known as a mud engineer and is maintained by trained drilling personnel.

DRILL PIPE; is a tubular designed to hold a certain weight called tensile weight. The drill pipe can be different sizes and grades, depending upon what depths you will be drilling. Drill pipe can be staged in different orders to prevent a tensile break due to exceeding the recommended Weight limits.

ELEVATORS; are hung from the beals and are used to hold the drill string when tripping in or out of the hole. They are certified to withstand a certain amount of weight. They are used to open, then close around the pipe so that you can open them when you are ready and remove the pipe from them and close them around the pipe when you need to move it.

HEAVY WEIGHT DRILL PIPE; is a medium weighted tubular, this is a heavy duty tubular that can handle a lot of weight and provide the drill string with more weight to drill or to stabilize the string to keep it centered as a pendulum.

LIGHT PLANT; is a Generator package designed to provide on demand Power to all Rig components at all times. These are a necessity on all Drilling Rigs.

MUD PUMPS; are the heart of a well, as it will pump the vital fluids needed to the well-bore and provide a constant movement down hole.

MUD TANKS; are large open top containers, which also provide a multitude of functions necessary to direct the drilling fluid to a certain place at ground level. They are also designed to separate the solids from the fluid so when the fluid reaches the suction, it is solid free and not contaminated.

RESERVE PIT; is a large pit dug into the ground that is designed to hold fluids and Drill Solids after the Well has been drilled.

ROTARY TABLE; is an assembly in the center of the rig floor which when engaged, rotates the drill string; via a collection of gears designed to rotate using the draw works or an electric motor for power.

SUBSTRUCTURE; is a base structure that can withstand a certified amount of weight. This is also the bottom of the drilling platform.

TOP DRIVE; is also known as a power swivel, is a housing of gears ran by hydraulics. It sets on a track mounted into the derrick and is used to turn the drill string and drill, ream or trip.

CHAPTER 21

TERMS AND DEFINITIONS

In the oilfield you will come across distinctive equipment, tools, and terminology that are not found in any other business. If you are new to the oil and gas industry, you will be learning and remembering some of these terms. It is sometimes overwhelming and can be frustrating at times. I hope this will help you understand some of these general terms and get you on the right track in becoming a well informed oil & gas professional.

Miscellaneous Terms in alphabetical order:

ABANDON; is a term used when production is stopped on a well that is depleted and no longer capable of producing profitably. This is the case when all other options have been explored.

ABANDON LOCATION; is when a situation dictates that all personnel immediately leave location meet at a pre-determined rally point. This is usually the situation when a blowout or sour gases have been discovered.

ACIDIZING; is the treatment of oil-bearing limestone or Hydrocarbon formations with a solution of hydrochloric acid and other chemicals to increase production.

AIR DRILLING; is the utilization of air to circulate and expel of medium from the well-bore, instead of using drilling fluids.

ANGLE OF DEFLECTION; is the angle or degree, at which a well is deflected from true vertical by means of directional drilling or other deflecting tools. This is also a term used to define the offset of a well-bore from a vertical point.

BLOWOUT ; is an Uncontrolled flow of gas, oil, or other fluids from a well during drilling operations due to excessive formation pressure, or due to using the wrong weighted drilling Fluid.

BREAKOUT; is a term used to unscrew and remove one section of pipe from another. Also a term used to describe beginning a career in the oilfield.

BREAK TOWER; is a term used when you have finished rigging up and you are ready to start drilling. This is also a term for when crews to stop working on a split schedule and work together.

BRING IN A WELL; a term used to describe the completion of a well and bring online into production.

CAPPED WELL; a well that is capable of producing but has been sealed for one reason or another; this could be due to surface work, or drilling too closely to the active well to allow it to produce safely.

CASING HEAD GAS; a term used when gas dissolved from crude oil migrates and emerges at the casing head when the pressure is lowered.

CAVING / SLOUGHING; is a term used to describe the result of the walls of the well-bore caving in on itself. This could be caused from using a mud weight not high enough to hold back the formation, also called heaving.

CATWALK; is a staging platform used to rest tubulars on before they are raised to the rig floor. It is also used to store tools onto after they have been lowered from the rig floor and laid onto the catwalk to be removed.

CELLAR; is a hole in the ground that the well-bore is in the center of, it is used to catch fluids from the well-bore and activity from above.

COAL BED METHANE; is a formation gas which has been formed in an ancient coal seam and bares methane gas from the decomposition over millennia. The coal bed methane is a clean gas and is easily retrieved for production.

CROOKED HOLE; is a term used when the well-bore (or hole) has deviated from the vertical position inadvertently, this could be from not taking surveys often enough and drilling out of optimum parameters.

DIRECTIONAL DRILLING; is a term used to describe the action of controlled angle drilling in a specific deviation and/or direction from a vertical point (inclination and azimuth). This will include horizontal wells and turnozontal wells. Note: any deviated hole beyond +5° is considered a directional hole.

DISCOVERY WELL; is a term used to define an exploratory well, in which the operator discovers a new oil or gas field that was not previously thought to be in existence; these are also called Wildcat wells.

DOG LEG; is a term used to describe any change in direction of a hole, rather it be intentional or accidental.

DOPE; is a form of thread grease used to lubricate the threads before a connection is made. This protects the threads and prevents unwanted early wear to the threads.

DOWN TIME; is a term used when the rig operations are temporarily stopped due to repairs or maintenance, these times result in the loss of revenue. Once the repairs or modifications are made the rig will then go back on the operator's payroll after being accepted.

DRILLING FLUID; is a mixture of oil, water or a synthetic blend where chemicals are added to the fluid to obtain the optimum weight, viscosity and yield point. These drilling fluids have been engineered by a trained professional and is used to carry cuttings to the top of the well-bore and then circulated and re-used. Air, natural gas, oil, synthetic oil and water are usually used as a base for these fluids.

DRY-HOLE; is a hole that did not produce the desired product, usually oil or gas.

DUAL COMPLETION; is a term used to describe the process in the completion, or fracing of a well, in which two separate formations may be produced at the same time. Also a term used to describe the duality of two wells on the same location which are being completed, or fraced at the same time.

FISH; is any undesirable object accidentally or purposely lost in the hole which must be removed before drilling can continue this could be a twisted off string of pipe or junk in the hole due to a tong die, slip die or tool being dropped in the hole.

FISHING; is a term used to describe the procedure that uses special equipment to remove a fish lost in the well bore; sometimes an over-shot, magnet or many other types of equipment is used in the retrieval.

FLOWING PRESSURE; is the pressure registered at the wellhead of a flowing well, during drilling operations, if not contained, or after the well has been drilled and is in the production stage.

GOING IN THE HOLE; is the act of placing drill pipe, or any other tubular used in the drilling or production phase being placed into the hole.

HOLE; is a common term for the well-bore, also called a bore hole.

JET THE PITS; a term used to describe cleaning out the entire mud tank, pit system of any and all drilling fluids and Solids accumulated during the drilling of the Well.

JUNK; is debris lost in the hole, due to a problem with down-hole equipment, or from someone dropping something inside of the well-bore and causing a metal in the hole problem.

KILLING A WELL; the act of bringing a well under control which has kicked or is threatening to blow out, this is also a process of ending the production of an active well.

LATCH ON; a term used to describe clamping the elevators onto the pipe or other tubular.

LAYING DOWN DRILL PIPE; is the act of pulling and disassembling the drill string and laying it down onto the pipe racks, in a trough, or;

using a hydraulic pipe handler, a lay down machine or a more primitive conventional method of chain and seal stop.

LOCATION; is a drill site or completion station site. A place where a well is being drilled or another site will be in the future. It is a permitted piece of property that is designed to house a drilling rig during drilling operations, pump station or injection site after the well has been drilled.

LOG; is a term used to describe a system designed to record well data, there are different types of Log's that measure a multitude of information. These range from a single temperature log, which checks for the height of cement, after it has been pumped, to a quad combo; which checks gamma, direction, density and a variety of other optional information.

LOST CIRCULATION; is a term used to describe the act of losing volume or mud, in any amount to an underground formation. This could range from a loss of 10% returns to losing all return and must be stopped to maintain circulation. Without circulation, it is impossible to expel the drill cuttings from the well-bore and you are unable to drill.

MAKE A CONNECTION; is a term describing the attaching of a tubular into the drill string which in turn lengthens the drill string and enables you to go deeper towards the goal of T.D.

MAKING HOLE; is a term used to describe the process of forward progress in the actual drilling operation.

MAKING A TRIP; is a term describing the process of pulling the drill string out and/or returning it into the hole, after a change has been made, or laying the drill string down after the operations have been completed.

MIXING MUD; is the process of mixing chemicals in preparation of the drilling fluids, from the mixture of water, oil, synthetic oil or other base fluid and other chemicals to produce a desired formula. This mixture is used to sustain the well-bore during the drilling operation and is also vital in the expulsion of drill cuttings from the well-bore to the surface.

OFFSET; is a term that describes a deviation created by the natural path of a bit to sidetrack in soft formations. This term is also used to describe the distance from the current well another well nearby, or a comparison made to a well in close proximity.

OPEN HOLE; is the uncased part of a well bore.

PENETRATION RATE; is the rate at which the drill bit progresses in the drilling of the formation. This is measured in two different increments, minutes per foot and feet per hour in the US. For our metric oil & gas professionals, the increments change to the metric system of measurement, to calculate the rate of penetration.

PERFORATE ; is a term used in the description of piercing or blowing holes in the casing within an oil or gas-bearing formation with a perforating gun or a hydro cutter which is lowered down the hole and fired electronically from the surface, this will open the casing up to the formation.

PRODUCTION; is the operation of bringing the payload to the surface; separating them and either storing them or transporting them to market or a plant, via a pipe line. Also the amount of oil or gas produced over a specific period is called a production measurement.

RIGGING UP; a term used to describe the assembling of a rig and getting it ready to start drilling and go on day rate (if applicable).

ROTARY DRILLING; is the method of drilling which the drill pipe is rotated to turn a bit, this is associated with the rotary table, or top drive, rotating the pipe and reaming.

SET CASING; is the process of the installation of steel pipe or casing in a hole, normally cemented in place by surrounding it with a wall of cement, this procedure can be performed several times during a well, to seal off the formation from the well-bore and the well-bore from the formation.

SIDE TRACKING; is the action of drilling past an obstruction in the hole, or kicking off to begin a curve for a horizontal or directional well. This can also be accomplished when reaming too fast and accidentally drilling a new hole, next to the existing one, without wanting to.

SINGLE; is the name of a single joint of drill pipe or tubular that is added to the string to lengthen it, or taken out of the string to shorten it by the range of pipe used.

SLIM HOLE DRILLING; is a term used to describe drilling the hole in a fashion in which the hole size is smaller than the conventional hole diameter. Thus enabling the operator to run a smaller casing and insure that it will be prolific to the formation in which it is intended. These holes are usually larger at the top part of the hole and then drilled smaller closer to TD.

SLUG; is a concoction of chemicals used with the active mud or drilling fluid to make it a mud heavy enough to force the fluid out of the drill string by gravity. This is usually performed before a trip, so that the fluid does not come to surface while tripping.

SPECIFIC GRAVITY; is the Ratio of weight of any substance in comparison to the weight of equal volume of another substance.

SPUD / SPUDDING IN; is a term used to describe the commencement of the actual drilling of a well, or also a term used to describe when the rig goes on day work or begins its operation on footage.

STAND OF PIPE; is a term of two, or three joints of pipe fastened together to produce a stand, this is only for rigs that are not singles. The single derrick rigs have single joints and are not called stands of pipe.

STRING; is the term used to describe the entire length of casing, tubing, or drill pipe, including the BHA. (I.e. string of casing, drill string or tubing string)

STUCK PIPE; is a situation where drill pipe, casing, or any other tubular becomes stuck and can't be worked in or out of the hole as desired by normal operations. This usually mandates a variety of tools and practices needed to help free the stuck pipe, so that the operations can continue.

SWABBING; is a term used to describe the operation of using a swab to bring the well fluids to the surface when the well does not flow naturally. In some instances, it is possible to swab a well by tripping too fast.

TIGHT HOLE; is a term used when drilling a well in which the information obtained is restricted and passed on to those only authorized to receive it. This information is closely guarded and civil suit can result if the information is given to any person unauthorized.

TORQUE; is the force that causes twisting or turning, e.g. the force generated by an internal-combustion engine to turn a vehicle's drive shaft.

TOTAL DEPTH (TD); is a term describing the maximum depth reached in a well, or when a stage of the well has been reached.

TOUR / TOWER; is the term of the scheduled work shift of a drilling crew. When the normal scheduled shift is changed, this is known as breaking tour.

TRAP; is a term used in the description of any geological structure which does not allow the migration of oil and gases through the sub-surface rocks, causing the hydrocarbons to accumulate into pools, this is usually a target for wells for production and also the target for storage wells, as these traps are a great area to store gas for later distribution.

TWISTED OFF; means to break a joint of drill pipe in two causing the loss of the Drill string and resulting in a recovery or fishing operation.

TWISTING OFF; is a term used when a roughneck or driller quits without notice while on tour.

WAITING ON CEMENT (WOC); is a term used to describe the time period that all well-bore operations are suspended; while the cement, used to hold the casing in the hole, cures and hardens for the specified amount of time.

WAITING ON ORDERS (WOO); is the term used to describe the time period that you wait on orders from the office or an engineer to direct you to your next operation. This could be a result of encountering an unforeseen formation, a change in the scope of the drilling operations due to a foreword plan or any number of things.

WILD CAT; is the term used to describe a well drilled in an unproven territory. These wells are sometimes called a wildcat well. They are also known as exploratory wells.

V-Door; is the term used to describe the operations slide (a slick piece of flat metal in a frame) that connects the catwalk to the rig floor. Almost all tools are brought up to the rig floor, or lowered down from the rig floor, using the v-door.

CHAPTER 22

STATE OF MIND

The state of mind from an oilfield worker's perspective is not unlike that of a soldier. As a person of either career, you feel as if you are the only one in the world that has to go through the things that you feel. Soldiers feel as if they are isolated for the most part from their family as they go off to fight for our freedom. They are responsible for a lot of things; but only hear from their superiors when the mission changes or they are to be reprimanded for a task poorly completed. In the oilfield, you will have to complete a wide variety of tasks without supervision as well. The only times you may hear from your supervisors are when there is a change in your job scope (mission.) This can be a lot to handle if you are not ready for the responsibility. Sometimes we feel abandoned if there is no one to share a laugh with or ask advice from.

This is more obvious of people that work on projects alone. You will for the most part always have someone to talk to in the oilfield; someone to communicate with is a positive aspect of the oilfield. You can work anywhere that you choose; this is your God given American right. So if you have anxiety about working alone, the oilfield is the perfect occupation.

The longer you perform a function, the better you get at performing that function. Keep your eyes open and your heart hungry; hungry for knowledge. As a young man, you found that you were better at some things than you were at others. The oilfield is just like anything else; the more you try the better you become. You should want to be the boss. You should want to have the knowledge that your supervisors have. This is what I mean about being hungry for knowledge; you must desire to know.

There are several steps in the oilfield. These steps can be mastered in a short time. If you work hard and try to be the best that you can be, then you will succeed. On the other hand, if you only give it half of the effort that it requires, you would probably be looking for a job more than you are working.

CHAPTER 23

THE TOTEM POLE

The steps or levels of the "totem pole" so to speak are; from lowest to highest.

ROUSTABOUT: is a general laborer who performs the lowliest of tasks in the oilfield as is available for travel from site to site to accomplish a task.

FIRE MAN: is used primarily on off shore rigs. He is responsible for the safety aspect of the drilling operation.

LEAD TONG HAND/ FLOOR HAND: is a general laborer. He must perform general functions assigned to him by the derrick man or driller.

CHAIN HAND: is a general laborer. He must perform any task assigned to him. He is next to motor man in command.

MOTOR MAN: is the floor boss and is a specialist. He has very specific knowledge of motors and mechanical equipment. He is next in command after the derrick man.

DERRICK MAN: is the supervisor of all floor men, chain men and motor men. He is responsible for the drilling mud and working in the derrick during trips. Being the second in command is a tough job and it usually takes years to accomplish this position.

DRILLER: is the main rig crew supervisor. He is responsible for the entire operation and the performance of his hands and the drilling of the well on his tour. He is also responsible for documenting all activities and insuring the safety of his hands.

TOOL PUSHER: is the primary supervisor over the entire rig and all of the rig's crews. He is responsible for the rig equipment, scheduling maintenance, inspections and coordinating with the company man. He is responsible for the rig's operation soundness and is over all of the drillers.

RIG SUPERINTENDENT: is the supervisor over several rigs (if applicable) and is responsible for all of the tool pushers, crews, equipment, logistics, cost and several other aspects of the operation. He is also the secondary liaison between the operator and the drilling contractor that he works for.

GEOLOGIST: is a specialist who studies rocks and formations. He/she are responsible for relaying the lithology information and the optimum placement of the well-path to the drilling engineers and company men.

ENGINEER: is responsible for the planning and completion of the well, he/she designs and makes modifications to the well plan accordingly.

COMPANY MAN: Is the top supervisor and is responsible for the operator's interest in the well. He documents and orchestrates all activities on the well site from logistics, location preparations, mobilization to and from the location, BOP testing, tubular inspections, ordering casing and cement and all third party contractors needed to achieve the goal of drilling and completion of the well.

These are the most common positions that you will hear about as an oilfield worker, excluding service hands that you will encounter. There are so many other people involved in the planning, mobilization and completion of an oil or gas well. As you spend time in and around the oilfield, you will encounter specialists in their own field. These people may offer you more information than you could imagine, or they may simply do their job and then leave. It is always good to "pick their brain" and see what you can learn from them.

I would like to take this opportunity to thank you for reading my book! If you are a newcomer… welcome to the oilfield. "Good luck to you and please, try to be safe!"

CHAPTER 24

SURFACE KILL SHEET

There are so many dangers as we continue to drill holes in these formidable grounds. We continue to drill deeper and drill longer horizontals as well. In this chapter, we will briefly cover the main methods used to kill a well.

One of these are the wait & weight method: wait to circulate and weight up your drilling fluids until you are able to pump the kill mud down the back side and kill the well.

Another is the driller's method: continue circulating and remove the influx from the well-bore and then circulate another circulation while building mud weight until the well is killed. This is also known as circulating under balanced. We will discuss and break down the wait & weight method.

The wait & weight method is the most common method that you will use, because this method allows the driller to shut in the well and make the necessary adjustments to the mud weight to kill the well. When we talk about killing the well, we are merely saying that we want to stop the influx or migration of gas into the well-bore.

This method is the most commonly practiced in the US and Canada, for good reason. The well is shut in and is not problematic any longer. The operation of the kill sheet will be taught to you as you gain experience in the oil & gas industry. You will notice this sheet in almost every doghouse for emergency purposes. Please study the kill sheet and familiarize yourself with the necessary information that will need to be entered in order to determine your kill weight needed to prevent the influx of any other well-bore gas or medium.

WAIT AND WEIGHT METHOD

1. Raise the mud weight in the suction pit to the desired kill weight mud value.

2. Monitor the shut in drill pipe pressure for a possible gas migration. Maintain drill pipe pressure constantly at the original shut in value if necessary.

3. After the KWM (kill weight mud) is ready, bring the mud pump on line according to pump start up procedure.

4. Maintain a constant pump speed during the kill procedure and adjust choke as needed to control drill pipe pressure as shown on the pump schedule of the kill sheet.

5. Follow the drill pipe pressure circulating schedule until the kill weight mud returns to surface.

6. If there are no other signs of a gas migration, return to the normal drilling activities.

CHAPTER 25

DESCRIPTIONS OF AIR HAMMER DRILLING

These percussion drilling tips have been written as a kind of hands-on guide for the oil & gas industry. It will help the driller, supervisor, and/or engineer who is using or planning to use down hole air hammers and bits. The objective of this manual is to give the reader guidelines and technical information that have been found to be helpful in planning and utilizing air hammer equipment and bits in oilfield applications.

Experience has shown that using these guidelines, medium hard to very hard formations can be drilled at rates of penetration up to 150+ feet per hour. These penetration rates are normally expected for the softest formations and were unheard of before the air hammer was introduced to the oilfield.

The major focus is to give you a basic understanding of air drilling techniques, suggested air volume requirements, air hammer designs, hammer bit designs, and other operational guidelines that have been found useful in the oilfield application. Also found within this manual are sections that address trouble-shooting, factors that affect P-rate, (rate of penetration) and deviation control techniques.

CHAPTER 26

HISTORY OF AIR HAMMERS

More efficient drilling techniques have been an important drilling component since the time of cable tool rigs. The high energy percussive action of the cable tool rigs were surpassed in drilling efficiency by the development of rotary rigs and roller cone bits in the early1900's. However, some form of percussion drilling continues to be used today to penetrate hard formations, particularly in mining applications, but more and more in the drilling of formations in difficult areas such as Pennsylvania, Ohio and West Virginia.

Roller cone bits require weight on bit to generate the crushing action on the formation. In soft or medium rock, the rotation combined with cone offset also generates a grinding action which contributes to the drilling efficiency. However in harder rock formations, the penetration action is reduced and the WOB is the main source of penetration rate. Thus, the efficiency of the roller cone bit decreases as the formation hardness increases because of the limited energy per cutter.

The optimum way to drill a hard rock formation is to have high frequency; high energy loads per cutter cross section and a rotary action that would move the cutters to unfractured formations between each successive load. This is precisely the goal of the air hammers that have been used in the mining industry since the early 1900's (commonly referred to in that industry as hammers). However, not until the mid 1960's did a high frequency low energy hammer make its way into the oilfield. These hammers were first attached to roller cone bits in an effort to increase the penetration rate over the conventional WOB and rotary applications in large surface holes. Higher rate of penetration resulted, but often the roller cone bits would fatigue from the increased loads and cause early bit failures, cone loss and barring failures. These results limited the use of air hammers with roller cone bits during the 1970's to a very specific market such as highly deviated areas, where lower WOB reduced the angle building tendencies that we see with the higher weight on bit.

In the mid 1980's, a new high frequency, high energy air hammer moved from mining into the oilfields of the northeast U.S. and Arkoma basin. Ran with a fixed-head bit (commonly known as a flat-bottom or hammer bit), the rate of penetration and total footage drilled per bit increased dramatically over roller cone bits for large surface holes. After some time, field engineers and bit salesmen realized that diamond enhanced inserts could be added to a hammer bit and improve the performance even further. Diamond enhanced inserts increased footage over standard carbide inserts by an average of 98%, increasing the R.O.P by 45% and reducing the overall cost per foot by 35%. It makes sense to drill as fast and efficiently as possible.

The diamond enhancement technology has helped the oil & gas industry's air drilling optimize the performance of every bit used. Some of the diamond technology and its history are shown below, just to give you an idea of its progress.

In the 1960's
Air drilling with roller cone bits

In the 1970's
Polycrystalline diamond cutters (PDC) developed for hard rock drilling

In the 1970's
Air drilling with roller cone bits on hammers

In the early 1980's
Air drilling with flat bottomed hammer bits and hammers

In 1984
Diamond enhanced inserts tested in roller cone bits to drill hard rock

In 1986

Diamond enhanced hammer bit became the oil & gas industry's standard for tough formations

This technology helped pioneer several companies to the front of the pack. This didn't only benefit the operators who used them, but also the bit companies who designed and perfected the technology. Today there are many companies who provide air hammers and are continually revamping the air hammer for specific drilling needs. The application of a diamond enhanced air hammer has even saved lives; a mine shaft collapsed in West Virginia recently where an air hammer was used to drill down and rescue the miners who were trapped.

CHAPTER 27

AIR DRILLING TECHNIQUES

There are three types of air drilling that we will cover in this chapter, they are; dust drilling, mist drilling and stable/stiff foam drilling.

The successful drilling of a well depends on the appropriate selection of the circulating fluid. When using a conventional mud system, lost circulation, formation damage, and high mud costs can occur. Air drilling techniques reduce the down-hole annulus pressure to inhibit the development of these familiar problems and can often result in enhanced production from the low pressure reservoirs.

(**Air drilling;** the use of air in the circulating system instead of drilling mud or other fluids in the expulsion of material from the well-bore.)

The primary application of air drilling is to drill low pressure, competent formations which give an influx when drilled conventionally. Over the past twenty years, air drilling techniques have been applied worldwide; successfully drilling for energy in many applications that were previously thought to be too problematic to effectively drill the well. That reasoning has since been rethought and there are new explorations taking place in these areas with a very brittle, hard or coarse formation.

The three general classifications of air drilling techniques are:

- Dust drilling

- Mist drilling
- Foam drilling (soap)

ADVANTAGES:

Air drilling techniques offer the following advantages, when compared to the use of conventional mud systems.

- Faster rates of penetration (ROP); (especially in harder formations) it seems that the harder the formation, the better the hammers perform.
- Improved bit performance (more footage per bit)
- Detection of low pressure zones. With fluid in the hole, it is harder to detect the gases that are trapped by the weight of the fluid. With air, it allows the gases to escape much easier.
- Elimination of lost circulation problems
- Lower mud material costs
- Faster return of uncontaminated cuttings for geological evaluation
- Minimized formation damage
- Improvements in deviation control (due to less weight on bit) the hole stays more uniform and straight with less weight on bit.
- Reduced environmental impact
- Lower overall drilling cost

DISADVANTAGES:

- Formation pressure control is minimal and, therefore, drilling is limited to geological regions where reservoir pore pressures are low.
- Drilling is limited to geological regions where the rock formations are mature and competent because there is little or no fluid pressure to support the borehole wall and prevent sloughing.
- There is limited ability to cope with significant volumes of water entering the annulus from water-producing formations.

I've seen these influx volumes at more than 100 barrels per hour.

- The bit gage can be greatly reduced during drilling, due to the constant friction on the bit and no fluid to assist in the cooling of the bit.
- The drill pipe can experience rather high wear due to sand blasting characteristics of a high annular stream flow.
- Air, unlike mud, does not cushion the drill string in the well-bore; making the possibility of drill string failures greater.
- There is a higher possibility of a dangerous down-hole fire. With no fluids to keep the gas at bay, it is more likely to influx the well-bore and could catch fire.

RATE OF PENETRATION:

The down hole circulating density of an air drilling system is low, compared to a typical mud system. The decreased circulating fluid pressure exerted on the well-bore increases the relief of the vertical and horizontal stresses residual in the formations. This reverse-pressure gradient significantly increases the drillability of the rock; as the down hole circulating fluid pressure is lowered below the formation pressure, the rock tends to explode at the bit tooth. Faster penetration rates result if there is sufficient circulating volume to clear the hole of cuttings. The increase in ROP may be 2-5 times the drilling rate of a conventional mud-drilled hole (without a mud motor). This can reduce the number of days required to complete a well, and reduce drilling costs.

BIT PERFORMANCE:

An air drilling system provides sufficient fluid turbulence to ensure proper cleaning of the cutting structure. Abrasive cuttings are carried away from the bit and into the annulus faster than with a conventional mud system. This lessens the re-grinding of drilled cuttings and improves bit performance (ROP). Elevated formation temperatures are common when drilling a geothermal well. One of the main factors affecting the performance of a bit is bearing life. As high formation temperatures are encountered, bearing life can be drastically decreased. An air drilling system supplies the bit with a cool stream of air that flows around the bearings, reducing the bearing temperature and increasing bit performance.

Decreasing the bearing temperature and reducing the re-grinding of drilled cuttings increases the footage that can be drilled for a given bit. This can result in fewer bits required to complete a well, reducing well costs.

DETECTION OF LOW PRESSURE ZONES:

The decrease in the bottom hole circulating pressure allows the depth of low pressure production entries to be recorded, while drilling. This information should be used to guard against the possibility of further damaging the zones as drilling continues.

DRILLING THROUGH LOST CIRCULATION ZONES:

Once lost circulation or production zones are encountered, drilling may continue through and beyond these low-pressure formations when air drilling. The operator may increase production from each well, by drilling deeper and encountering new production zones. The existing air circulating system may or may not have to be changed to maintain full circulation. A properly engineered air drilling system will permit a rapid conversion from one technique to another, without any excessive delay.

MUD MATERIAL COST:

The down-hole circulating fluid pressure may exceed the formation integrity pressure, when drilling into a low-pressure zone with a conventional mud system. This may induce fractures, allowing drilling fluid to be lost into the porous formation. Higher drilling costs result because of the increased amount of mud materials required to replace the lost mud. The lower circulating pressures of air drilling systems usually permit effective drilling through low-pressure zones, minimizing drilling fluid losses, and permitting full returns to the surface. By decreasing loss of circulation, the number of drilling days, and the products required to service the circulating system, the mud and drilling costs can be reduced by using an air drilling system.

MINIMIZED FORMATION DAMAGE:

The use of air drilling techniques can minimize formation damage and enhance production from low-pressure wells, when compared to a conventional mud drilled well. If the circulating fluid pressure is less than the formation pressure, there is little chance that circulating fluids and cuttings will invade and damage producing zones. Some geothermal operators have indicated that wells completed with conventional drilling fluid systems have less geothermal production, when compared to wells drilled with air drilling systems in the same area. These operators feel that low bottom-hole circulating pressures decrease invasion, and cooking of drilling fluid and cuttings in the high temperature fractures.

DUST DRILLING:

Compressed air is injected into the standpipe and circulated through the drill string in much the same way as conventional mud. The term dust was chosen because the cuttings return to the surface as a cloud of dust. The dust technique is used when drilling dry formations, or where any water-influx is slight enough to be absorbed by the dust stream. The drilling air is used to cool the drill string and the bit. After compression, the temperature of the air injected into the hole will be higher than the temperature at ambient conditions. As the air travels down the drill string the air is heated to approximately the temperature of the surrounding drill string and surrounding formation.

When the air passes through the jet nozzles the air velocity increases and a pressure drop occurs. The pressure drop causes expansion of the air, which results in a decrease in air temperature. This temperature decrease cools the bit and the down-hole motor's bearings, stator and rotor. As the air travels up the annulus, the air is then re-heated to the temperature of the surrounding formation.

If lubrication of the drill string and bit is desired a lubricant must be injected into the air stream. There are several products that perform this function. The application of a lubricant decreases torque and increases bit life. If soap is used as the lubricant, there will be an increase in the carrying capacity of the circulating fluid. Fluid in this capacity is described as; smooth and graceful in a way that seems relaxed. Even though the drilling fluid is air, it is still fluid in movement. Dust drilling is the ultimate progression from a high to a low density drilling fluid. Bottom-hole pressures slightly exceed the value of the air column pressure head plus the weight of the entrained cuttings. This allows for maximum relief of the vertical and horizontal stresses residual in the formations. Where feasible, dust drilling generally offers the fastest penetration rates and best overall economy.

HOLE CLEANING:

The lifting power of an air drilling system is proportional to the circulating density, and to the square of the velocity. The density and corresponding suspension properties of an air stream are much lower than those of a conventional mud system. Therefore, the annular velocity is the primary factor in transporting the cuttings to the surface.

Air volumes that generate annular velocities of 3k ft/min are normally adequate to dust drill. However, when penetration rates exceed 60 ft/hr, or when cuttings are large or become wet, higher annular velocities may be required to effectively clean the hole.

EROSION:

A high annular velocity may cause erosion in soft formations. If the use of an air drilling technique causes erosion of the well-bore, the addition of a stabilizing agent or changing air drilling techniques may be required to minimize this problem. Erosion of the drill string can also be caused by the high annular velocities and temperatures generated when steam zones are encountered. The ingress of steam results in high local velocities, estimated in some cases to be as high as 10k ft/min. Since corrosion accelerates erosion, the injection of barrier type chemicals will inhibit this type of erosion

CORROSION CONTROL:

Corrosion control should be considered before beginning the use of an air drilling technique. When drilling through formations with acid contamination (CO_2 and H_2S), corrosion could be problematic. Mixtures of hydrogen peroxide (H_2O_2) and caustic soda (NaOH) can be used to solidify and precipitate the H_2S contamination at the surface. An organic phosphate scale inhibitor can prevent the deposition of alkaline earth metal scale on the drill string.

A protective barrier placed on rock and metal surfaces can help protect these surfaces from erosion and corrosion. There are two types of products available for low or high temperature service. A blended amine designed to reduce erosion and corrosion of metal surfaces in high temperature geothermal environments has increased the life of drill pipe. This inhibitor is premixed with water and injected down-hole with the air normally after steam zones have been encountered.

CHAPTER 28

MIST DRILLING

This technique is used where the amount of water-influx is high enough to prevent dust drilling, but not enough to cause hole cleaning problems. The term mist was chosen because a pre-treated drilling fluid is injected with the air, and the combination returns to the surface as a mist. A small quantity of water containing a foaming agent (soap) is injected into the air stream at the surface, with the water mist being carried in the air in what is a continuous air system.

This technique offers increased drilling rates and economy over that of a conventional mud drilled hole. The lower bottom-hole circulating pressure exerted on the well-bore allows for greater relief of the vertical and axial stresses residual in the formations. Like dry air drilling, this system relies on the annular velocity of the air for cuttings expulsion out of the hole. Essentially, the equipment for successful dust or mist drilling applications is the same, the principle difference being an increase in the air volume requirements by 30%, and the injection of a pretreated drilling mud.

HOLE CLEANING:

Switching to a mist drilling technique requires an increase of at least 30% in the air volume. The additional volume is needed to overcome higher frictional losses caused by wet cuttings adhering to the drill string and hole, higher slip velocities of larger wet cuttings, and transportation of the heavier wet air column. The mud is injected with the air stream to disperse the cuttings and inhibit them from adhering to the drill string and hole.

Although injection pressures of 100 to 200 psi are normally enough for dust drilling, pressures exceeding 350 psi can be encountered while mist drilling. Pressures of 1,250 psi may be required when large amounts of fluids are present in the annulus. The rate of fluid intrusion will dictate the amount of air and fluid that must be injected to efficiently clean the hole.

Formation fluid influxes of up to; 150 bbl/hr (100gpm) have been successfully mist drilled.

The addition of a foaming agent reduces the interfacial tension of the water and cuttings in the hole and allows small water/cutting droplets to be dispersed as a fine mist in the returning air stream. This allows the cuttings and water to be removed from the hole without formation of mud rings and bit balling.

Proper amounts of water and soap must be added to achieve a nominally continuous flow of foam and cuttings and adequate separation of the cuttings. Obtaining the proper combination of water and soap is a trial and error process. Good starting points are:

- 6 - 12 BPH water (4-8 gpm)
- .5 - 4 GPH soap (0.1% to 0.25% by volume in the water).

These requirements are a function of the type and volume of influx water. Many produced brines are effective de-foamers, requiring use of additional soap. Produced oil requires a special type of soap.

To determine the proper amount of water and soap to be injected, several "rules of thumb" are helpful:

- Air volumes for mist tend to be greater by 30% than dry air drilling.
- Pressures generally run at 200 - 400 psi for mist (vs. 100 - 300 psi dry air drilling).
- Insufficient air/soap leads to slugging, with attendant pressure increases (surges).

CORROSION CONTROL:

The fluid properties required for mist drilling are lower than a conventional mud system. Chemical treatment is needed to minimize corrosion caused by the additional fluid and air. Basic corrosion control is provided by maintaining the pH of the mud system above 10.5, and treating any hardness or carbonates with the appropriate chemical. Hydrogen sulfide and carbonate scale are treated in much the same way as in a conventional mud system.

Corrosion coupons should be run in the saver and crossover sub to monitor the type and rate of corrosion. The selection of the best chemical treatment or corrosion control product should be based on the coupon analysis.

If H_2S is encountered, the first line of protection is to maintain the pH at or above 11. To precipitate out the sulfides, a source of zinc should be added based on the level of contamination and the type of fluid injected.

To reduce carbonate corrosion, lime is used to treat out the carbonates, and some excess is maintained to buffer against this type of corrosion.

Oxygen corrosion is the most difficult to combat in an air drilling system, because the air supplies large quantities of oxygen to the wet circulating system. There are several types of chemicals that can be used to minimize this type of corrosion.

Scale is a common problem with some type of fluids. Using an alkaline fluid and treating the carbonates and hardness with the appropriate chemicals will greatly reduce the tendency of scale to occur. If the fluid circulating system is correctly pre-treated, corrosion can be maintained at an acceptable level.

CHAPTER 29

STABLE AND STIFF FOAM DRILLING

The removal of drilled cuttings from low pressure formations is a serious problem, particularly when permeability is high and the rocks are unconsolidated; when conventional methods are used, solids can be forced back into the formation. Since the reservoir pressure is extremely low, these contaminants stay in place and restrict permeability with a subsequent reduction in productivity. A low density circulating fluid minimizes contamination of the producing zone by mud materials and cuttings. Decreased circulating pressures allow the drilling of severe loss zones with minimum fluid loss. A proven method for lowering the hydrostatic head is to use the stiff foam drilling technique.

Stiff foam is a mixture of water, foam, appropriate mud additives, and compressed air.

Foam is generated at the surface and injected in the drill string as the circulating fluid. Stiff foam can be used when dust or mist drilling techniques would not be practical because of economical, mechanical, or other reasons.

WHEN TO USE STIFF FOAM DRILLING:

- To drill severe loss circulation zoned, particularly those with wet or weeping formations.
- To drill water sensitive shales which tend to slough when they are mist drilled.
- To drill unconsolidated formations or producing zones.

- To cope with situations where not enough air is available for large diameter holes, remoteness of location, or economics.

ADVANTAGES:

- Low hydrostatic pressure is exerted against the well-bore, reducing the invasion of drilling fluids and cuttings thereby minimizing formation damage.
- Full circulation can be obtained in holes where it has been impossible to maintain returns with conventional fluids.
- Oil and water zones can be readily identifies by analyzing the foam returns at the blooey line.
- Low annular velocities of approximately 100 to 300 ft/min permit the drilling of unconsolidated formations without the problems associated with hole washout.
- Lower fluid volumes enhance the ability to drill in-gauge, large diameter holes. The mud products are used to provide hole stability, carrying capacity, foaming characteristics, and corrosion control. They also decrease the tendency of the air to break-out of the foam in the annulus. The air is used to reduce the down-hole circulating pressure.

Properly mixed foam weighs 2 to 4 lbs/cu. ft. When the foam is compressed down hole it exerts minimum hydrostatic pressure with little or no fluid loss to the formation. Foam has excellent carrying capacity for cuttings, about 7-8 times that of water.

The foam mixture cannot be re-circulated. Environmental concerns may result when large amounts of foam are present at the surface.

Stiff foam drilling does not work well when large formation flows are encountered. As the formation fluid enters the well-bore the foam strength is reduced, decreasing the ability of the circulating system to clean the hole of cuttings. To combat this problem an increase in the circulating rate and material concentration is required to strengthen the foam, which increases the drilling costs.

There are many types of foaming products on the market that will perform well in fresh water, salt water, oil, and gas producing zones. It is better to purchase a quality foamer rather than a bargain foamer. When drilling problems are encountered the additional cost of the quality foamer will be offset by better performance down-hole. Cuttings removal is strictly dependent on the stability of the foam. If the foam returns and cuttings are watched constantly, they give adequate warning of impending trouble. When the foam is muddy it is apparent that the hole is enlarging. As the hole enlarges the annular velocity drops and the foam ceases to lift the cuttings as efficiently. As long as an adequate air volume and foam mix is available to lift drill solids and fluid entries, hole integrity is the only limiting factor in successful foam drilling of low pressure reservoirs.

MIXING:

Stable foam is mixed at the surface, preformed, and circulated a single time through the hole. This pre-foaming eliminates problems with contamination. (Salt water, oil, sulfides, and steam have all been successfully handled with this technique). It readily separates into its gas and liquid components at the surface pit. In mixing stable foam, compressed air or gas is fed through a foam generator. The water/detergent solution is prepared in a blender in a general range of 0.1 to 1.0 parts foaming agent to 100 parts of solution (1% to 2% foaming agent by volume). Foam is formed by pumping the water/detergent solution through an injection tube into the air/gas stream. The preferred range of gas to liquid ratio is 3/50 ft3/ gal, which can be adjusted according to down hole requirements. Injecting water into the air stream during stable foam drilling provides a mechanism for introducing other chemical additives to meet individual requirements of the well.

With stable foam drilling applications, annular velocities as little as 100 ft/min are seen regularly. These lower annular velocities contribute to reduced hole erosion and large cuttings. Since stable foam drilling systems are air internal systems containing high concentrations of foam and water, the potential for a down-hole fire is virtually eliminated. This fact and the ability of the system to provide excellent water and cuttings transportation, make stable foam systems one of the most versatile of all reduced pressure drilling systems.

CHAPTER 30

AIR COMPRESSORS

There are two basic types of compressor equipment used in air drilling applications, screw- and piston type air compressors. During air drilling operations the compressor uses local atmospheric air. The compressor unit intakes a specific volumetric rate of atmospheric air, then compresses the volume to the required pressure level and injects this air into the standpipe manifolds. A booster may be required to increase the pressure of the air flow from the compressors, as they are limited to their pressure output.

The piston-type compressor is the type generally used for air drilling operations. This type of compressor has the important characteristic of responding to pressure variations without altering the volumetric flow rate from the machine. Increased pressure requirements are met with increased power to produce a higher pressure at the exit. In air drilling the volumetric flow rate is very important to hole cleaning; the field equipment must have the capability of producing a relative constant volumetric flow rate under a variety of pressure conditions. There have been many disputes in the past regarding the manner in which the volumetric output of a compressor unit is reported.

FREE AIR (ACFM):

Free air is the actual amount of air (acfm) delivered by the compressor unit without correction for temperature, pressure, and humidity. A value reported in free air (acfm) must be accompanied by the pressure, temperature, and humidity for that value to have significance.

STANDARD AIR (SCFM):

Standard air (scfm) is the amount delivered by the compressor adjusted for pressure, temperature, and humidity variations for standard conditions. Correcting free air to standard air allows the use of a set of standard conditions as the reference point for comparison between various locations. If a value is reported in standard air (scfm) the pressure, temperature, and humidity do not have to be provided when reporting the flow rate.

SCREW COMPRESSORS:

There are many screw compressor manufacturers, each with their own designs. For this reason there isn't a generic equation to calculate the actual output from any given screw compressor unit. The rating given by the manufacturer must be used; however, if there is a change in the reference conditions, there is an accompanying change in the volumetric output of the unit. Thus it is extremely important to monitor flow rate on the exit side of these compressors.

The screw type compressor is less efficient than the piston type unit at higher pressure levels. As the air pressure requirement increases, the machine will screw through itself, losing volumetric output. The screw compressor requires the aid of booster equipment to meet higher pressure requirements. This translates into higher fuel costs to deliver the same air volume rate.

NOTE: Using an assumed efficiency for screw or piston type compressors in all situations may result in inadequate flow rates and/or bailing velocities. Thus it is recommended that a flow meter be used to measure actual air volumes.

CHAPTER 31

ESTIMATING FLOW RATES

Volumetric efficiency is defined as the ratio of the actual delivered capacity (measured at inlet temperature, pressure, humidity, and gas composition) to the piston displacement.

The accepted specific heat ratio for air is k = 1.4, the total cylinder clearance is %Cl = 17%, and the internal losses are generally estimated at L = 15%. A graph can be produced to show the theoretical capacity of the piston type compressor unit versus the outlet pressure.

SUGGESTED AIR VOLUMES FOR PERCUSSION DRILLING:

Since air is a compressible gas, its behavior is quite different from that of drilling fluids. At constant temperature air behaves according to.

$P_1V_1 = P_2V_2$ @ Constant Temp

This physics law states that air volume is inversely proportional to the confining pressure; stated another way, in which as air pressure increases its volume decreases. When dealing with mud this concern can be ignored since the change is very slight.

With this in mind we need to understand how (SCFM) standard cubic feet per minute compressor ratings were established. All compressors are rated in SCFM which is the volume of air at the intake of the compressor at standard atmospheric conditions (14.696 psia and 59°F with a specific weight of 0.0765 lbs/ft3.)

ORIFICE METERING OF AIR:

In 1977, the (ANSI) American National Standards Institute adopted a standard to calculate the air flow rate measurement through an orifice plate. To eliminate the necessity for individually calibrating the measuring elements, detailed rules have been established governing the fabrication of the component parts. If there is any question to the validity of the flow data, then inspection of these elements should take place.

Flow meters should be a standard part of any air drilling package but often it is a good idea (especially if validity is questioned) to inspect the meter to eliminate any questions about air volumes if hole cleaning problems occur.

CALCULATION OF AIR VOLUME REQUIREMENTS:

Air volume calculations for percussion drilling are somewhat similar to mud hydraulic calculations with a down-hole motor. In the previous discussion, we determined the difference between the rated and actual air volumes delivered by both screw and piston type compressors.

The starting point for a drill string calculation is to determine the air volume required to clean the annulus, based on hole size, drill pipe OD, ROP, and experience. Once air volume is known, surface pressure is calculated by summing the pressure losses that occur in each section of drill pipe, annulus and across the hammer and bit

Step: 1). Calculation of the pressure at the bottom of the pipe section (P) AP Inside the annulus in air drilling:

PAP depends on the following quantities:

- Annulus pressure at the surface, PAS (lb/ft2 abs) = Patm
- Penetration Rate, K i.e., the rate at which cuttings are generated (ft/hr)
- Flow Rate, Q (scfm)

- Hole Diameter, DH (ft)
- Outer Diameter of Pipe, DPO (ft)
- Length of the Pipe Section, LP (ft)
- Average Temperature in the Pipe Section, Tavp (R)

Step: 2) Determination of bailing velocity:

Q = Flow Rate
TAP = Temperature at the bottom of the Pipe Section (R)
TAC = Temperature at the bottom of the Collar Section (R)
PAP = Annulus Pressure at the bottom of the Pipe Section (lb/ft2abs)
PA = Annulus Pressure at the bottom of the Collar Section (lb/ft2abs)
DH = Hole Diameter, DH (ft)
DPO = Outer Diameter of Pipe (ft)
DCO = Outer Diameter of Collar (ft)

Step: 3). Calculation of the pressure at the bottom of the collar section (P) AC inside the annulus in air drilling:

PAC depends on the following quantities:

- Pressure at the bottom of the pipe section in the annulus, PAP (lb/ft2 abs)
- Penetration Rate, K i.e., the rate at which cuttings are generated (ft/hr)
- Flow Rate, Q (scum)
- Hole Diameter, DH (ft)
- Outer Diameter of Collar, DCO (ft)
- Length of the Collar Section, LC (ft)
- Average Temperature in the Collar Section, Tavc (R)

Step: 4) Calculation of pressure above the hammer (PB) in air drilling:

PB depends on the following quantities:
- Annulus Pressure at the bottom of the hole, P P A AC ≈ (lb/ft2 abs)

- Flow Rate, Q (scfm)
- Hammer Geometry
- Choke Diameter
- Ambient Air Temperature, T Tavc ≈(R)

The pressure drop across the hammer (P) H is a complex function of the above quantities and is usually published by the manufacturer for different flow rates.

Step: 5) Calculation of the bore pressure at the top of the collar section (P)BC:

PBC depends on the following quantities:

- Bore Pressure above the hammer, PB (lb/ft2 abs)
- Flow Rate, Q (scfm)
- Inner Diameter of Collar, DCI (ft)
- Length of the Collar Section, LC (ft)
- Average Temperature in the Collar Section, Tavc (R)

Step: 6) Calculation of the standpipe pressure i.e., bore pressure at the top of the pipe section

(P) BP:

PBP depends on the following quantities:

- Bore Pressure above the Collar section, PBC (lb/ft2 abs)
- Flow Rate, Q (scfm)
- Inner Diameter of Pipe, DPI (ft)
- Length of the Pipe Section, LP (ft)
- Average Temperature in the Pipe Section, Tavp (R)

Step: 7) If BV < BV min, Then:

- Increase the SCFM to satisfy minimum BV requirements.
- Look up hammer operating pressure vs. increased SCFM.
- If pressure is too high for the hammer consider opening bypass choke.
  (Appendix A - Hammer Comparison Chart).
- Then rerun pressure calculations, if necessary.

Step: 8) ensure that the air compressors are capable of handling the standpipe pressure expected.

CHAPTER 32

PARTICLE DYNAMICS

A particle falling under the influence of gravity will accelerate until the drag force on the particle just balances the gravitational force. The particle will continue to fall at a constant rate known as the terminal velocity. The terminal velocity of a spherical particle can be estimated with a simple equation, use these as your basis.

- U_t = terminal velocity (feet/sec)
- g = acceleration of gravity (feet/sec 2)
- d_p = diameter of particle (feet)
- q_p = density of particle (pound/feet3)
- q_f = fluid density (pound/feet3)
- c_d = drag coefficient (dimensionless)

The formula that you just performed shows that the terminal velocity of a cutting is inversely proportional to the fluid density. As the relative fluid density decreases, the terminal velocity will increase. Using this logic, the terminal velocity of a typical cutting in air will be very high compared to the terminal velocity of the same cutting in mud. The velocity of the air must exceed the terminal velocity of the cutting to move upward in the annulus. To use air as the circulating fluid requires a high annular velocity to successfully clear the hole of cuttings.

If we consider a particle in a rising stream of fluid, and let U_f be the upward velocity of the fluid, then the slip velocity or the velocity of the particle relative to the fluid (U_s) is given by: $U_s = U_f - U_t$

There are four possible flow profiles:

1. $U_f = O$, $U_s = -U_t$ (particle falling in a stationary fluid at its terminal settling velocity)
2. $U_f = U_t$, $U_s = O$ (particle suspended in the fluid)
3. $U_f = U_t$, $U_s = O$ (particle settling at relative velocity of $U_t - U_f$)
4. $U_f = U_t$, $U_s = O$ (particle moving upwards with the fluid at a relative velocity of $U_f - U_t$)

From the above equations, we can calculate the value of the annular velocity that is greater than the terminal velocity of the cuttings. As cuttings are generated at the bit, they will rise rapidly past the drill collars. Once the cuttings clear the top of the collars and enter the annulus between the drill pipe and the well-bore, the fluid velocity decreases considerably because the cross sectional area increases. Due to this reduction in fluid velocity, the point that the cutting is most difficult lift is located at the top of the drill collars.

Particles that are larger than the critical diameter capable of being lifted by the circulating fluid will tend to accumulate in this section. They will fall back and be re-ground between the drill pipe and the well-bore, drill collars and the well-bore, the bit, or by collisions with other particles. This process will continue until the larger particles are broken into a size such that their terminal velocity is less than the fluid velocity above the collars and they become easier to expel from the well-bore.

Where the air drilling has failed; very often the reason has been an insufficient air volume, or velocity, to clean the hole at the fast drilling rates. As the well deepens, more air is necessary to maintain the velocity needed to bring the cuttings to the surface. The increase in the air requirements stem from higher friction losses due to the lengthening fluid column, and density increases due to the increasing weight of the column of drilled solids, which result in higher down-hole pressures and consequently lower bottom hole velocities. If no additional compressor capacity is immediately available, air requirements may be reduced by decreasing the area of the annulus; this could be obtained by either decreasing the hole size or increasing the drill pipe diameter. A smaller annulus imparts higher velocities for a given injection rate.

CHAPTER 33

RULE OF THUMB CALCULATIONS FOR AIR DRILLING

Determine bailing velocity and scfm requirements:

To estimate the minimum recommended bailing velocity use the following simplified formula:

BV = 528 D1/2 C1/2

Where: BV = Bailing Velocity (ft/min)

D = Rock Density (lb/ft3) (see appendix)

C = Diameter of Rock cuttings (in)

For this example, let's assume a large sandstone (sand weight is 165 lbs/ft3) cutting with a size of 1/2" so that we are assured of cleaning smaller chips from the hole. Inputting these values:

BV = 528 (165)0.5 (0.5)0.5 = 4795 ft/min (at 1000' depth)

For depths greater than 1000' a rule of thumb is to increase air volume by 5%, compounded per 1000', to compensate for the compression of air due to hydrostatic pressure at depth and pressure drop in the annulus: 1093 cfm * (1.05)5 = 1395 cfm

CORRECTING FOR ALTITUDE AND TEMPERATURE:

1395 cfm / 1.198 = 1164 scfm

Estimate the actual volume delivered by compressors:

Now that the volume of air required to produce the recommended minimum bailing velocity has been calculated, determine whether the output of the available compressor(s) is sufficient. Note that the output of a compressor will vary based on its condition and on ambient air conditions:

- Compressors become less efficient with age: as a rule of thumb, apply an 80% correction factor to the compressor's rated flow rate.

  Example: 1000 cfm x .80 = 800 cfm

- The density of air changes with temperature and altitude

EXAMPLE:

- Pennsylvania - Altitude = 3000 feet
- Ambient temperature = 100°F
- Drill Bit Size - 7 7/8"
- Drill Collar Size - 6 1/4"
- Drill Pipe Size = 4 1/2"
- 3-850 cfm rated screw compressors - total 2550 cfm correcting for efficiency, available air volume is 2550 cfm .80 = 2040 cfm

Correcting for altitude/temperature 2040 cfm, 1.198 = 1703 scfm

Calculate the approximate actual bailing velocity:

First, apply the correction factor as above to estimate air volume at depth:

1703 CFM / $(1.05)_5$ = 1334 cfm

Rule of thumb air volume requirements for dust drilling (scfm)

Note: Increase by 30% for mist or directional drilling

Note that the air volume needed for hole cleaning may be much higher than that required to operate the hammer if excess air is not bypassed it may cause excessive hammer operating pressure, resulting in bit or hammer failure. To prevent this situation, a choke is often installed in the hammer to bypass excess air. In situations that require unusually high air volumes (i.e. large hole size drilled with relatively small drill pipe), it may be necessary to run a bypass sub above the hammer. These are some of the rule of thumb calculations that will help in determining the volume required to lift a particle and expel it from the well-bore.

Chapter 34

Hammers

The pin up connection: the A.P.I. (American Petroleum Institute) connection that connects the hammer to the drill string. This is the connection that will screw into the drill collar, bit sub or crossover (XO) sub.

The typical connection sizes are:

4" 2 3/8 Reg.

6" 3 1/2 Reg.

8" 4 1/2 Reg.

12" 6 5/8 Reg.

Check valve (back flow valve): rubber-coated spring-loaded poppet valve which stops flow back through hammer when air supply has been stopped.

Feed tube (control rod): air supply tube that transfers air to the piston timing ports. It generally also contains the choke, which can be used to aid in hole cleaning and utilization of available air supply.

Piston: the only moving part of the hammer, the piston travels at a high frequency and transfers energy to the bit and formation. Usually the heaviest internal part of the hammer, the piston may travel at 800 to 1600 beats per minute.

Bit retaining rings (lock rings): a split ring which is captured between the driver sub and the top bit bearing to keep the bit engaged in the hammer and provide the freedom for the bit to travel from off-bottom to on-bottom positions.

Driver sub (chuck): internally splinned sub attached to the hammer that engages with the splinned section of the bit to transmit rotational force from the hammer and drill string to the bit.

Description of air hammers operation:

The typical air hammer operation begins with the hammer off bottom and bit extended out to the blow position. The piston is in the down position resting on the bit striking face; piston ports are not aligned with the feed tube windows. Air bypasses all timing ports and flows through the piston ID, out bit ports and up the annulus.

The hammer is lowered to bottom and the bit slides up in the hammer moving the piston up simultaneously. The lower chamber ports in the piston align with the feed tube windows and the lower chamber is charged, starting the piston in the upward stroke. Once the bottom of the piston travels past the blow tube (foot valve) the lower chamber is able to exhaust through the bit. At this point the feed tube windows are no longer aligned with the lower chamber ports.

Due to its momentum, the piston continues to travel upwards, aligning the upper chamber ports with the feed tube windows and charging the upper chamber. The pressure in the upper chamber overcomes and then reverses the momentum of the piston, driving it downwards. The piston travels downwards with great velocity until impacting the bit, sending its impact energy as a stress wave through the hammer bit and into the formation. After striking the hammer bit, the piston then rebounds and the cycle is initiated again. This cycle repeats until the drill string is picked up, allowing the bit to drop to the blow position, at which time the piston ports are not aligned with the feed tube and the piston will not cycle.

HAMMER BIT DESCRIPTION:

FOOT VALVE (BLOW TUBE): an aluminum tube, which is pressed into the upper bore of the bit. This tube mates in the bottom ID of the piston, seals the lower chamber and starts the piston in an upward direction after it strikes the bit. The foot valve also exhausts the lower chamber after the piston clears it to start the next cycle.

BIT STRIKE FACE: the uppermost surface of bit that is perpendicular to the shank. When impacted by the piston, energy is then transferred from the piston through the strike face to the bit and ultimately to the formation.

UPPER BEARING SURFACE: the area supported by the upper bearing which helps to align the bit with the driver sub.

BIT RETAINING AREA: the upper area of bit with the smallest outside diameter which allows the bit to be captured by the bit retaining rings and also allows the bit to travel in and out of the operating positions (on bottom & off bottom)

DRIVE SPLINES: an externally splinned section of bit that mates with the internally splinned section of the driver sub to transfer rotational force from the drill string through the hammer and then to the bit.

LOWER BEARING SURFACE: the outer diameter closest to the bit head that helps support the bit in the driver sub when on bottom.

SHANK: the portion of the bit between the striking face and the lower bearing surface is referred to as the shank.

FISHING THREADS: the external rope threads that are in the top of the head and are designed to be used with a mating fishing tool. These are used in fishing a broken hammer bit out of the hole.

DIAMOND ENHANCEMENT: diamond enhanced inserts placed on the outer edge of the hammer bit to help stabilize and prevent drilling severely under gauge hole.

CHAPTER 35

MUD MOTORS

Let's discuss the use and practicality of down-hole motors. The down-hole mud motor revolutionized the drilling industry in many ways. The invention and technical adaptation of the down-hole mud motor made it possible to drill long laterals and with the current technology, there is almost no limit to the lateral length of a well-bore. Remember this, distance is subject of friction. This means that you are only restricted to a certain lateral length due to friction on the well-bore's walls; and of course, the hard lines determined by the leasing agreement.

The mud motor was not always so clear and cut in its destination. The mud motor's predecessor was a rotary steerable tool that used a bent motor housing to determine its positioning underground. Once a bent sub was set, the directional driller must then keep the orientation throughout the entire drilling operation. If the orientation was even a fraction of an inch off at surface, the well-bore could be drilled outside or the lease lines and even outside of the pay zone. The next step in the mud motor evolution was the addition of the adjustable motor housing. This made the orientation a little simpler, but the directional driller must still maintain a constant watch on the orientation of the drill string.

The next innovation was the cure all to the orientation of the motor and the destination of the well path. This "super application" was the MWD (Measure While Drilling) tool; this technology isn't new by any means. It was first used by the US Navy in the 1940's during military operations. It was designed to place torpedoes onto a target with pinpoint accuracy.

Used in many different applications until the pulsing was configured to optimize well drilling capabilities in the early to mid 1980's. After MWD was mastered, it was only a matter of time before the designers made it even better, more user friendly if you will. There are many different facets to the MWD, the directional drilling industry's capability and the professionalism that accompany them. We will cover the basics in this chapter.

ECONOMICS:

The increasing reliability of drilling motors in combination with improved drill bit designs and measurement while drilling (MWD) systems now present operators with alternatives to rotary drilling in an increasing number of applications.

It is generally acknowledged that an effective down-hole motor, matched to the proper drill bit and formation parameters, provides better rates of penetration than any rotary drilling or rotary steerable applications could obtain. In addition to increasing the rate of penetration, a mud motor allows a reduction in drill string rotary RPM, which reduces wear on the casing, wear and fatigue of the drill string and topside rotating components; such as a kelly or top drive system. It also provides more effective control over deviation and doglegs during the drilling process which will save cost and boost productivity in the well itself.

Drilling with a motor can be more fuel efficient because, the hydraulic power that is required to drive the down-hole motor and drill bit may be less than the mechanical power required to drive a rotating drill string with the associated friction losses. This, as we all know due to the cost of operational boundaries, will save money in fuel and time.

MOTOR SELECTION:

The selection of the motor to be used is as much a part of the solution as the motor itself. If we choose the wrong speed of motor or the wrong yield of the motor, we could be hindering ourselves as much as not using one at all. The choice of motors is very important due to the drilling parameters and performance. For example; if your well plan is designed on a BUR (Build Rate) of 10°/100' then you would assess the formation and make a decision on which motor you would use, and the bend that you would place in the adjustable housing, to yield the desired builds. If you place a motor which is not aggressive enough in the hole, your yield wouldn't be satisfactory and you would fall short of the target landing. On the other hand, if your build is too aggressive, you would over shoot your landing and lose valuable production area of the well known as (vertical section). This can be avoided by trial and error, when using offset wells and previous well plans in the area.

For instance; if you drill a well that is designed to be drilled vertically to a KOP (Kick off Point) of 6,784' and it is designed with a 12° per 100' curve and then a 3,500' lateral section. You would plan to have at least three motors on location. The first motor, unless you are using a straight hole motor, would be your curve motor. This motor would have to be configured to yield 12° per 100'. This could be done by setting your adjustable setting on 2.18° or even 1.83° if the formation will let you build to the desired rates.

In some instances, a much more aggressive setting is needed. If you are drilling in a very soft, organic formation such as black shale, you may need to consider setting the motor more aggressively to achieve the desired builds. Some formations fall off due to the turbulent flow at the bit. In this instance, the formation is so soft and porous that it simply melts away as the force of the fluid hits it. In this situation, there are a couple of things that can help you obtain your builds and inevitably help you land the curve in the desired vector.

When your motor is not yielding the desired builds and you are already drilling with the assembly, you can slow your pump rate down. This prevents the clearing of the formation in front of the bit and allows more weight to be applied in the desired direction. If you are building at 11° left and the desired build rates needed are 13's, you may even pull out of the hole and dial the motor setting up to a 3° setting to allow you to catch up to your curve design.

Engineers and well planners usually take into consideration, the fact that a formation has yielded less than desirable rates on offset wells. If this is the first well in an area, you may need to discuss the options that will help you obtain your desired builds. We are all in the business to complete a well faster and more efficiently than the next guy.

DUMP SUB:

The dump sub allows drilling fluids to bypass the motor section and fill the bore of the drill string when tripping into the hole. It also allows the bore of the drill string to drain when tripping out of the hole. When no dump sub is used, a wet trip out of the hole will occur. At low circulation rates, a spring holds a ported piston in the upper position, exposing ports in the dump sub body which allow drilling fluids to flow into or out of the drill string while tripping.

When the rig pumps are started, the flow through the piston bore causes a pressure drop across the ports in the piston. This forces the piston down, overcoming the spring force and closing the ports which in turn directs the drilling fluid through the motor. When the rig pumps are stopped, the spring forces the piston up, opening the ports. When this port functions properly, the design is a great tool to help keep drilling fluids in the well-bore and saves money due to the loss of expensive drilling fluids

POWER SECTION:

The drive is like a long symmetrical boat propeller operated in reverse. Drilling fluids are pumped through the assembly causing a rotor to turn and apply a rotary motion and torque to the drill bit, through the articulated driveshaft and the output shaft in the sealed bearing assembly. The power section consists of a helical shaped rotor (much like the screw type compressor in chapter 30) running inside the stator.

The pitch length of the stator cavity is longer than the pitch length of the rotor. The dissimilarity in the shapes of the rotor and stator produces wedge shaped cavities that are sealed along their edges. The pressure that is produced as drilling fluid is pumped through the motor section causes the rotor to turn and the cavities to move forward in the direction of fluid flow. The 1 to 2 lobe configuration, used in some high-speed motors, has a helical shaped rotor with a circular cross section (1 lobe). The elastomeric liner opening of the stator is oblong in cross section (2 lobes), and is molded in a helical shape with a pitch length twice that of the rotor pitch length

The multi-lobe configuration, employed in low speed, high torque motors, uses a rotor with a multiple-lobed cross section that also forms a helix. The elastomeric liner in the stator has a cross section containing one more lobe than the rotor. Its pitch length is longer than the rotor's pitch length by the ratio of the number of stator lobes divided by the number of rotor lobes.

EXAMPLE: a 7 to 8 lobe configuration has 7 lobes on the rotor, 8 lobes in the stator; and a helical pitch length of the stator equal to 8/7 times the pitch length of the rotor. The number of stages of a motor is the length of the stator elastomeric liner divided by its pitch length.

These drives permit accurate determination of the bit speed and bit torque on bottom from the rig floor at any time. The output torque is directly proportional to the pressure drop across it. This is a straight line relationship and can be determined from the standpipe pressure gauge. The drive's speed is proportional to the circulation rate. At a constant circulation rate, the speed drops off slightly as the torque and pressure increase. The circulation rate can be read from the pump stroke counter. The stator is threaded on both ends with a box that uses a designed thread. It connects to the dump sub above and to the bent housing below. The rotor has a box connection that connects to the upper universal joint of the articulated driveshaft assembly.

ARTICULATED DRIVESHAFT:

The articulated driveshaft assembly converts the eccentric or processional motion of the rotor into concentric rotation for input to the sealed bearing assembly. It also accommodates any angle set on the adjustable bent housing (or fixed bend housing) and carries the thrust load from the rotor caused by the pressure drop across it.

The assembly consists of two universal joints connected by a driveshaft. The upper joint connects to the rotor and the lower joint connects to the sealed bearing assembly. Both universal joints are lubricated, sealed, and pressure balanced.

SEALED BEARING ASSEMBLY:

Sealed bearing assembly motors are a common and almost demanded design in the oil & gas industry. The sealed bearing assembly transmits the rotation of the rotor, through the articulated driveshaft assembly, then to the drill bit. It carries the compressive thrust load created by the weight on bit, and the radial and bending loads developed while directional or steerable drilling. It also carries the tensile thrust load produced by the pressure drops across the rotor and the drill bit, as well as any load caused by back reaming.

The motors radial bearings and thrust bearings are sealed in an oil chamber balanced to the hydrostatic pressure. The thrust bearings are high capacity and there is no need to balance the hydraulic thrust load to bit load with the motor. The high capacity radial bearings readily withstand side loads caused by drilling with a deflection device or uneven cutting action along the drill bit periphery. The lower connection is an API regular bit box connection.

STABILIZERS:

Most motors are available with a thread on the outside of the sealed bearing assembly to accept straight or spiral blade screw-on stabilizers or screw-on offset pads. A protector is installed over this thread when stabilizers or offset pads are not being used. This is an industry standard for stabilizers, however they are not always desired. In some situations, a stabilizer will cause more problems than they will cure. They are a good addition when they are used in the proper application, but are not always the best choice. They are designed to stabilize the drill string and stop the lollop or flop of the string in the formation. But in a formation that has a tendency to slough, the stabilizer would more than likely cause drag and allow the string to get stuck, or pack off.

OPERATION:

No matter whether the application is a correction run, directional kick-off, sidetrack extended reach, horizontal well, or you're on a core run; careful consideration of all parameters will go a long way in ensuring the successful execution of the planned task.

Hydraulic requirements, circulating fluid data, R.P.M. requirements, and formation characteristics must be addressed to ensure the proper selection of the applicable motor. Most down-hole motors are shipped from the service center with all tool connections made up to the proper torque, and all components inspected and tested for satisfactory operation. Low speed/high torque motors are shipped with the rotor bore plugged unless otherwise specified. All motors are shipped with a protector covering the screw-on stabilizer thread unless a screw on stabilizer is ordered. When ordered in advance, the screw-on stabilizer is installed at the service center before shipment.

You should set the motor in the slips and install a safety clamp or wedding band. Remove the lift sub and make up motor to the kelly or top drive. Remove the safety clamp and slips and lower the motor until the dump sub is below the flow nipple, but visible so you can watch the results. Start the rig pumps slowly; fluid should flow out of the dump sub ports. Increase the pump rate slowly until the dump sub closes. Leave the pumps running and make note of the circulation rate and stand pipe pressure when the dump sub closes.

With the pump running and the dump sub closed, check to ensure that there is no drill fluid leakage through the ports. It is advisable to increase the pump speed in two or three steps, to the maximum circulation rate expected down hole, and note the circulation rate and standpipe pressure in each case. Shut down the pump; the dump sub may not open due to a pressure lock in the short hydraulic test circuit. If this occurs, bleed off the pressure to permit the dump sub to open. Insure that the motor is rotating and everything looks good. Make up the drill bit to the proper torque in the bit breaker and the rig tong placed on the output shaft directly above the bit. Do not put rig tongs on the sealed housings. Inspect the output shaft for any indication of an oil leak. If the tongs are placed onto the sealed housing, it can be damaged and cause a motor failure.

TRIPPING IN:

The drill string with a straight motor installed can be run into the hole normally. When using a bent sub, or a non-zero angle in the adjustable housing, be careful passing the motor through the blowout preventers, casing shoes, liner hangers, ledges, or key seats to ensure that the motor or drill bit does not hang up and become damaged. Do not run into bottom, or fill, as it could plug the bit or damage the motor.

STARTING THE MOTOR:

Begin circulating off bottom with the bit turning freely. Perform circulation and pressure tests at the same circulation rates as the prior surface test, and note the readings. The pressure will be higher due to the restrictions of the drill string components added. The off bottom pressures noted may be higher than calculated. This is caused by bit drag on the side of the hole due to the bent sub, adjustable housing angle and stabilization.

DRILLING:

After a short hole-cleaning circulation period, slowly lower the bit to bottom. When bottom is tagged, the standpipe pressure gauge will show an immediate increase. Increase the bit weight slowly to achieve the desired build up rate and/or rate of penetration. Do not exceed the recommended maximum differential pressure across the motor.

The off-bottom pressure is the total system pressure (read on the stand pipe gauge), from the standpipe, through the drill string, the annulus, and back to the drilling nipple, while circulating with the bit off bottom (i.e. zero weight on bit). Periodically recheck the off bottom pressure. The standpipe pressure will slowly increase after hole cleaning due to the hydraulic energy required to lift the cuttings.

The torque applied to the bit while on bottom is directly proportional to the difference between the on bottom and off bottom pressures (i.e. there are no friction losses through the rotating drill string). An increase in the weight on bit produces an increase in torque. As the bit drills off, the weight on bit decreases and correspondingly the pressure and torque decrease. The standpipe pressure gauge can therefore be used as a torque indicator.

The range of motors permits selection of the correct motor to provide the optimum combination of bit speed, bit torque, and circulation rate for maximum rates of penetration. When the drilling conditions permit, the rotary can be engaged. Running into bottom can damage thrust bearings, and excessive over pull on a stuck bit can damage off bottom bearings in the sealed bearing assembly. The motors should be serviced after a maximum of 150 operating hours, under ideal drilling conditions.

Drilling conditions other than ideal, such as excessive bit weight, corrosive drilling fluids or rotating with high bend settings will reduce this interval accordingly.

REACTIVE TORQUE:

The drill bit attached to the mud motor at the bit box turns in a right hand, or clockwise direction, if viewed from the drill floor. There is a reaction that occurs when the bit is placed onto the bottom of the hole; the result is reactive, counter clockwise (or left-hand) torque produced as a result of the torque applied to the bit. This anticlockwise torque must be considered when establishing tool face orientation and can be calculated by relating the: Difference of on bottom pressure and off bottom pressure as relative to the anticlockwise torque.

The difference between off bottom free spinning pressure and actual on bottom operating pressure is known as the differential pressure. This pressure is one of the parameters that you will be using to determine the actual weight to bit that is being applied.

Directional drillers can get an indication of the reactive torque by the measurement while drilling (MWD) equipment, and can adjust and lock the rotary table in order to accommodate the desired tool face direction. If you are attempting to slide at 90° and the reactive torque is causing you to lose 10° of tool face, you can make an adjustment and slide in the desired direction by adding the 10° loss to your hold by sliding at 100°.

In most applications the use of measurement while drilling (MWD) or steering tools to provide real time surface read-out of azimuth, inclination and tool face is much more reliable than the single shot method of orienting.

STALLING THE MOTOR:

If the drill bit is overloaded, the motor will stall. An increase in standpipe pressure will occur and penetration will cease. When a stall out occurs, the drilling fluid deforms the stator elastomeric liner and flows through the PDM drive without turning the rotor. Bit stalling should be avoided, but when it occurs, it should be quickly remedied. Excessive circulation through a stalled PDM drive or repeated stalling will seriously damage the stator elastomeric liner and other components within the motor. If the bit is picked up off-bottom when in a drilling mode, the trapped torque within the drill string will be released uncontrollably, potentially causing damage to down-hole components or causing connections to back-off. This is especially true when a stall out has occurred. If a stall condition occurs the following procedure should be followed as soon as possible.

1. Shut down the rotary table immediately.

2. Release trapped torque slowly using the rotary brake.

3. Lift the bit off bottom

4. Shut the pumps off, if necessary.

OVER-RUNNING THE BIT:

Rotating the drill string with any positive displacement motor in a stalled condition may cause the upper portion of the motor (and drill string) to over-run the bit. This condition may damage the stator elastomeric liner. High torque/low speed multi-lobe motors are most susceptible to this type of damage.

ROTARY RPM:

Rotating the drill string while subjected to bending loads produces fatigue loading on the motor. These bending loads can be produced even when using adjustable bend settings that are within the recommended values. The drill string rotary speed should therefore be limited to 70 RPM to reduce the cyclic loading on the motor as recommended by the manufacturer.

MOTOR PRESSURE DROP:

Exceeding the recommended operating maximum differential pressure across the motor will reduce the stator life. Circulation rates exceeding the recommended values also reduce the rotor and stator life. To understand the conditions affecting the pressure drop across positive displacement drilling motors, the following should be recognized:

1. The pressure drops across the dump sub, bent housing, articulated driveshaft, and bearing mandrel of the sealed bearing assembly is dependent on the circulation rate only (i.e. torque has no effect). This pressure drop increases as the circulation rate increases.

2. The pressure drop across the rotor and stator increases linearly as the torque increases, assuming a constant circulation rate.

3. The effect of mud weight alters the pressure drop across the motor at no load. However, it has a negligible effect on the pressure increase due to the torque "on bottom".

BIT PRESSURE DROP:

Continuous excessive pressure drops across the bit can cause early seal failure in the sealed bearing assembly. The bit pressure drop should be limited to 1,500 psi (10,000 kPa) for continuous drilling. However, motors can be configured to operate with bit pressure drops in excess of 1,500 psi.

Drilling fluids:

Drilling fluids with a pH below 4 or above 10 can cause damage to the stator. Circulation through the rotor and stator can minimize this damage and should therefore be maintained when operating in drilling fluids close to the limits of this pH range. Allowing the drilling fluid to stagnate will aggravate the problem. Pumping acid through a motor can seriously attack the plated components. The motor should be flushed and serviced as soon as possible.

Drilling fluids containing chlorides can reduce rotor and stator life due to corrosion, especially at elevated temperatures. Special attention should be paid to the internal coatings when the chloride concentration is in excess of 30,000 PPM. The motor should be flushed and serviced as soon as possible if it has been exposed to chlorides. Drilling fluids with a density of more than 16.7 PPG (2.00kgf/l) will cause abnormal erosion of motor internals due to suspended materials within these fluids. Well mixed medium to fine lost circulation material can be used without plugging a motor or cause motor damage. If coarse lost circulation material is to be used, a circulating sub should be installed above the motor assembly to bypass the motor. The lost circulation material can also become an issue with the MWD tool, as these orifices are a certain diameter and can only allow so much material to be passed through before plugging occurs.

Oil Based Drilling Fluids:

Down hole motors can be successfully used in oil based mud if the operating temperature is below the aniline point of the oil. However, oil based fluids will deteriorate the elastomeric stator liner and consequently it is recommended that the stator be relined after it has been run in an oil based mud. The aniline point (i.e. temperature) of an oil is an indication of its tendency to cause swelling of elastomeric parts (e.g. stator, seals), and is a measure of the oil's content. The lower the aniline points of the drilling fluid, the greater the swelling tendency.

The aniline point gives a measure of the solvent power of a petroleum product for aniline, which is related to its solvent power for many materials. This solubility increases with increasing temperature.

Operating a motor in an oil based fluid at temperatures above the oil's aniline point allows the aromatic portion of the oil to permeate and swell the stator elastomeric liner and reduce its hardness and strength. The swelling increases the interference between the rotor and stator and results in heat build-up that leads to rapid destruction of the stator elastomeric liner. Power sections with larger clearances are available to minimize the effects of swelling. Elastomeric compounds seem to perform better in mineral based mud systems than in diesel or oil based systems. Low toxicity oil base systems are easier on elastomers because they contain fewer aromatics.

Plugging Off:

The motor may plug off with cuttings entering the drill string through the filter plugs in the dump sub ports. To prevent this occurrence the hole should be circulated to achieve bottoms-up before running in the hole with a motor. This may also occur upon breaking connections when drilling cement or unconsolidated sands, etc. As the annulus loads up with cuttings, and the kelly is broken off, U-Tubing occurs, (i.e. the pressure in the annulus exceeds the pressure in the bore due to different fluid densities). If this occurs, immediately make the kelly back up and resume circulation to ensure that the hole is cleaning properly. In some cases it may be necessary to blank off the dump sub to obtain the optimum circulating force required to reverse the U-Tube effect.

DEVICES:

Directional drilling or sidetracking operations traditionally used a bent sub or kick sub placed above the dump sub. A disadvantage of the bent sub above the motor is that it places the bend too far off bottom or too far from bit to bend and the drill string should not be rotated.

Bent housings placed between the drive section and lower bearing section place the bend closer to the bit, tilting the bit and bearing housing axis in relation to the motor, minimizing the bit wall drag. Motors containing bent housings can be rotated. The disadvantage of conventional bent housings is that their angle cannot be changed in the field.

The adjustable housing has the advantages of placing the bend close to the bit, and it can be rotated. It is easily adjustable from straight to 3° in 12 increments (or 2° in 12 increments, or 4° in 18 increments), on the rig floor while it is securely in the elevators. The adjustable housing eliminates the need to select a bent housing angle before a motor can be assembled and shipped. Motors contain a screw-on stabilizer thread on the lower sealed bearing assembly to enable the motor to be run slick with the adjustable housing, or with field installable stabilization as required.

STEERABLE SYSTEMS:

The desired angle is set in the adjustable housing sufficient to alter the hole course with the drill string not rotating and the tool face oriented. When the drill string is rotated with the motor operating, the system drills straight ahead. The broad range of circulation rates, bit speeds, and bit torques available with steerable down hole motors make them suitable for use with journal bearing and roller tri-cone bits, PDC bits and diamond bits. The measurement while drilling (MWD) system software, bit selection, and operation of the total system has made the mud motor a perfect tool in the oil & gas industry.

Now that we have covered the basics of the down-hole motor, its uses and its optimum performance, you are better prepared to make a wise choice in your selection. Choosing the optimum motor for your application will be pertinent to the well cost and the drilling days of your well. If you choose your motor, bit and directional company wisely, you could begin to set new performance records in any area.

CHAPTER 36

GEOLOGY

Numerous deposits of oil shale, ranging from Precambrian to the Tertiary age, are present in the United States. The three most important deposits to date are in the Eocene Green River formation in Colorado, Wyoming, and Utah, the Devonian-Mississippian black shales in the eastern United States, which include the Marcellus Shale and the Barnett Shale in central Texas. Oil shale associated with coal deposits of Pennsylvanian age is also in the eastern United States. Other deposits are known to be in Nevada, Montana, Alaska, Kansas, and elsewhere, but these are either too small, too low grade, or have not yet been well enough explored to be considered as resources for the purposes of mass production. Because of their size and grade, most investigations have focused on the Green River, Marcellus and the Devonian-Mississippian shale deposits.

GREEN RIVER FORMATION:

Lacustrine sediments of the Green River formation were deposited in two large lakes that occupied 65,000 (km2) in several sedimentary-structural basins in Colorado, Wyoming, and Utah during early through middle Eocene time. The Uinta Mountain uplift and its eastward extension, the Axial Basin anticline, separate these basins. The Green River lake system was in existence for more than 10 million years during a time of a warm temperate to subtropical climate. During parts of their history, the lake basins were closed, and the waters became highly saline.

In addition to fossil energy, the Green River oil-shale deposits in Colorado contain valuable resources of sodium carbonate minerals including nahcolite ($NaHCO_3$) and dawsonite [$NaAl(OH)_{2CO3}$]. Both minerals are commingled with high-grade oil shale in the deep northern part of the basin. In 1974, it was estimated the total nahcolite resource at 29 billion tons. It was also estimated that nearly the same amount of nahcolite and 17 billion tons of dawsonite. Both minerals have value for soda ash (Na_2CO3) and dawsonite also has potential value for its alumina (Al_2O3) content. The latter mineral is most likely to be recovered as a by-product of an oil-shale operation.

Eastern Devonian-Mississippian Oil Shale:

Black organic-rich marine shale and associated sediments of late Devonian and early Mississippian age underlie about 725,000 km^2 in the eastern United States. These shales have been exploited for many years as a resource of natural gas, but have also been considered as a potential low-grade resource of shale oil and uranium. Over the years, geologists have applied many local names to these shales and associated rocks, including the Chattanooga, New Albany, Ohio, Sunbury, Antrim, and others.

The black shales were deposited during Late Devonian and Early Mississippian time in a large epeiric sea that covered much of middle and eastern United States east of the Mississippi River. The area included the broad, shallow, interior platform on the west that grades eastward into the Appalachian Basin. The depth to the base of the Devonian-Mississippian black shales ranges from surface exposures on the interior platform to more than 2,700 m deep along the depositional axis of the Appalachian Basin.

The Late Devonian Sea was relatively shallow with minimal current and wave action, much like the environment in which the Alum Shale of Sweden was deposited in Europe. A large part of the organic matter in the black shale is amorphous bituminite, although a few structured fossil organisms such as tasmanites, botryococcus, foerstia, and others have been recognized. Conodonts and linguloid brachiopods are sparingly distributed through some beds. Although much of the organic matter is amorphous and of uncertain origin, it is generally believed that much of it was derived from planktonic algae.

In the distal parts of the Devonian sea, the organic matter accumulated very slowly along with very fine-grained clayey sediments in poorly oxygenated waters free of burrowing organisms. It has been estimated that 30 cm of the upper part of the Chattanooga Shale deposited on the interior platform in Tennessee could represent as much as 150,000 years of sedimentation.

The black shales thicken eastward into the Appalachian Basin owing to increasing amounts of clastic sediments that were shed into the Devonian sea from the Appalachian highland lying to the east of the basin. Pyrite and marcasite are abundant authigenic minerals, but carbonate minerals are only a minor fraction of the mineral matter.

The oil-shale resource is in that part of the interior platform where the black shales are the richest and closest to the surface. Although long known to produce oil upon retorting, the organic matter in the Devonian-Mississippian black shale yields only about half as much as the organic matter of the Green River oil shale; which is thought to be attributable to differences in the type of organic matter (or type of organic carbon) in each of the oil shales. The Devonian-Mississippian oil shale has a higher ratio of aromatic to aliphatic organic carbon than the Green River oil shale, and is shown by material balance Fischer assay's value to yield much less shale oil and a higher percentage of carbon residue.

When hydro-retorting the Devonian-Mississippian oil shale can increase the oil yield by more than 200 percent of the value determined by the Fischer assay value. In contrast, the conversion of organic matter to oil by hydro-retorting is much less for Green River oil shale, about 130 to 140 percent of the Fischer assay value. Other marine oil shales also respond favorably to hydro-retorting, with yields as much as, or more than, 300 percent of the Fischer assay value.

Marcellus Shale Orientation:

The Marcellus Shale is black shale of Middle Devonian age that underlies much of Pennsylvania, New York, Ohio, West Virginia and adjacent states. Geologists have long known that the Marcellus contains natural gas, however, the depth of the rock unit and its low permeability made the Marcellus an unconventional exploration target.

Within the past few years, two technologies, hydro-fracing and horizontal drilling have been tested in the Marcellus resulting in some of the most productive wells in the eastern United States. These developments triggered an explosion of drilling and leasing activity in the areas above this rock unit.

The potential of the Marcellus is significant. It is thought to contain about 50 trillion cubic feet of natural gas - enough to supply the entire United States for two years with a wellhead value of one trillion dollars. The Marcellus is also the closest natural gas to the high demand markets of New York, New Jersey and New England.

Shale is a fine-grained sedimentary rock that forms from the compaction of silt and clay-size mineral particles that we commonly call "mud". This composition places shale in a category of sedimentary rocks known as "mudstones". Shale is distinguished from other mudstones because it is fissile and laminated; laminated means that the rock is made up of many thin layers and fissile means that the rock readily splits into thin pieces along the laminations.

Shale breaks into thin pieces with sharp edges. It occurs in a wide range of colors that include: red, brown, green, gray, and black. It is the most common sedimentary rock and is found in sedimentary basins worldwide

Uses of Shale:

Some of these shales have special properties that make them important resources. Black shales contain organic material that sometimes breaks down to form natural gas or oil. Other shales can be crushed and mixed with water to produce clays that can be made into a variety of useful objects.

Conventional Oil and Natural Gas

Black organic shales are the source rock for many of the world's most important oil and natural gas deposits. These black shales obtain their black color from tiny particles of organic matter that were deposited with the mud from which the shale formed. As the mud was buried and warmed within the earth some of the organic material was transformed into oil and natural gas.

The oil and natural gas migrated out of the shale and upwards through the sediment mass because of their low density. The oil and gas were often trapped within the pore spaces of an overlying rock unit such as a sand stone. These types of oil and gas deposits are known as conventional reservoirs, because the fluids can easily flow through the pores of the rock and into the extraction well.

Although drilling can extract large amounts of oil and natural gas from the reservoir rock, much of it remains trapped within the shale. This oil and gas is very difficult to remove because it is trapped within tiny pore spaces or adsorbed onto clay mineral particles that make-up the shale.

Unconventional Oil and Natural Gas:

In the late 1990s natural gas drilling companies developed new methods for liberating oil and natural gas that is trapped within the tiny pore spaces of shale. This discovery was significant because it unlocked some of the largest natural gas deposits in the world.

The Barnett Shale of Texas was the first major natural gas field developed in a shale reservoir rock. Producing gas from the Barnett Shale was a challenge. The pore spaces in shale are so tiny that the gas has difficulty moving through the shale and into the well. Drillers discovered that they could increase the permeability of the shale by pumping water down the well under pressure that was high enough to fracture the shale. These fractures liberated some of the gas from the pore spaces and allowed that gas to flow to the well. This technique is known as hydraulic fracturing or hydro-fracing.

Drillers also learned how to drill down to the level of the shale and turn the well 90 degrees to drill horizontally through the shale rock zone. This produced a well with a very long pay-zone through the reservoir rock. This method is known as horizontal drilling.

Horizontal drilling and hydraulic fracturing revolutionized drilling technology and paved the way for developing several giant natural gas fields. These include; the Marcellus Shale in the Appalachians, the Haynesville Shale in Louisiana, the Barnett Shale in Texas and the Fayetteville Shale in Arkansas. These enormous shale reservoirs hold enough natural gas to serve all of the United States' needs for twenty years or more.

Everyone has contact with products made from shale. If you live in a brick house, drive on a brick road, live a house with a tile roof or keep plants in terra cotta pots you have daily contact with items that were probably made from shale.

Many years ago these same items were made from natural clay. However, heavy use depleted most of the small clay deposits. Needing a new source of raw materials, manufacturers soon discovered that mixing finely ground shale with water would produce clay that often had similar or superior properties. Today, most items that were once produced from natural clay have been replaced by almost identical items made from clay manufactured by mixing finely ground shale with water.

Cement is another common material that is often made with shale. To make cement, crushed limestone and shale are heated to a temperature that is high enough to evaporate off all water and break down the limestone into calcium oxide and carbon dioxide. The carbon dioxide is lost as an emission but the calcium oxide combined with the heated shale makes a powder that will harden if mixed with water and allowed to dry. Cement is used to make concrete and many other products for the construction industry.

Oil Shale:

Oil shale is a rock that contains significant amounts of organic material in the form of kerogen. Up to 1/3 of the rock can be solid kerogen. Liquid and gaseous hydrocarbons can be extracted from oil shale but the rock must be heated and/or treated with solvents. This is usually much less efficient than drilling rocks that will yield oil or gas directly into a well. Extracting the hydrocarbons from oil shale produces emissions and waste products that cause significant environmental concerns. This is one reason why the world's extensive oil shale deposits have not been aggressively utilized.

Oil shale usually meets the definition of shale in that it is "a laminated rock consisting of at least 67% clay minerals," however; it sometimes contains enough organic material and carbonate minerals that clay minerals account for less than 67% of the rock.

CHAPTER 37

BLOW OUTS

A blow out is an uncontrolled flow of reservoir fluids into the well-bore, and sometimes catastrophically to the surface. A blowout may consist of salt water, oil, gas or a mixture of these. Blowouts occur in all types of exploration and production operations, not just during drilling operations. If reservoir fluids flow into another formation and do not flow to the surface, the result is called an underground blowout. If the well experiencing a blowout has significant open hole intervals, it is possible that the well will bridge over (or seal itself with rock fragments from collapsing formations) down hole and intervention efforts will be averted.

In the years that I have been in the oil & gas industry, I have only been on one major blow out. A blow out is the sudden influx of gas or volatile fluid into the well bore. These types of catastrophes can be avoided by utilizing the proper blow out prevention equipment and inspecting them regularly. The blow out preventer (BOP) is only one part of the equipment used to avoid this very dangerous situation.

Your first line of defense is knowledge. Having the knowledge of the possibility of there being an over pressurized zone in the formations that you will be drilling into. This information is sometimes obtained through the blood and lives lost from people who have drilled through the formation before. Seismic data is also a very good way to know what formations are in the path of your well bore. If there is a possibility of encountering an unstable or over pressurized zone, please be overly cautious.

Your BOP will be your primary defense mechanism and should

be inspected regularly and repaired without delay if one of the many components is found faulty. A BOP is comprised of many components. The primary component is the ram type preventer.

A ram preventer is a steel casted body which houses gears and the ram itself. When the hydraulic gear is pressurized, the rams close onto the pipe to seal the well-bore off and stop the flow of gases or fluids from escaping. A ram type preventer uses a variety of inserts to perform its function.

These types are pipe rams, blind rams and shear rams. The pipe ram closes around the pipe to create seal, preventing any gases or fluids from escaping. The blind rams are used to seal the well in the event that there is no pipe in the hole at the time of the influx of well-bore gases or fluids. The shear rams are used to shear any pipe in the event that it becomes too violent for your surface equipment to handle it safely. The shear ram cuts the tubular in half and seals the well completely.

As you may assume; you will usually be running a different size casing than your drill pipe's O.D. so after you trip out of the hole, you'll need to close the blind rams to seal the well off from the environment. The blind rams are placed below the pipe rams. They are placed in this order to allow you to change out the pipe rams in the event that you run casing or change the tubular size. After the pipe rams are changed out, the BOP (stack) will need to be re-tested for your safety.

The second component used on the BOP is the annular preventer. Thus is not like the ram type preventer and is a bladder type. The bladder type preventer seals of the annulus as the hydraulic fluid is pumped into the bladder, expanding it and sealing the annulus off; hence the name annular preventer. The annular preventer does not withstand the force that a ram type preventer does and only holds approximately 1,500# of force. The annular preventer is better used as a temporary solution in an emergency.

The next component used will be your manual choke valve, HCR (Hydraulic Closing Ram), choke manifold and gas buster. These are all subjected to a high amount of pressure and volume in the event of an influx (kick). Everything that will have pressure on it during a kick must be tested and certified for your safety.

Now on the other side of the stack, you'll have the kill side. The kill side is the offense side of a blow out. You are able to close the preventers, open the choke and divert the fluids to the gas buster and flare line. But left uninterrupted, the pressures could build higher than the pressure rating of the BOP equipment.

The kill valve will be left until the kill mud is weighted up and ready to pump. Then the kill valve will be opened and the kill mud will be pumped down the annulus to first equalize the pressure and then to suppress it with the heavy mud weight. Once the heavier mud weight is placed on top of the kick, it will lose its force and soon dissipate. It is compared to the weight you are able to lift. The lighter the weight, the easier it would be to lift it. When more weight is added, it becomes more difficult to lift.

The surface lines and mud pumps will be used to pump the kill mud down the hole. Therefore, they will have the pressure from the well-bore on every inch of the lines and the pump. They must also be tested and certified for your safety.

The BOP inspection report must be posted in the operator's office (shack) or the tool pusher's shack. This is required by all state and federal agencies. OSHA requires that the stack or BOP & BOPE (BOP Equipment) be tested prior to the start of any well, after any change is made to the BOP or BOPE, or every 27 days; whichever is more frequent.

A blow out is very violent; once it has ignited there is little that is able to be done to stop the fire from raging. There are specialists who are the industry's leader in putting out a rig or oilfield fire. They usually end up imploding the well to seal it off and extinguish the fire; but there are many ways that these professionals are able to stop them from igniting or if they have already ignited, they can stop them from continuing to burn.

CHAPTER 38

HELPFUL EQUATIONS AND FACTORS

CONVERSION

MULTIPLY	BY	TO OBTAIN
Acres	43560	Square feet
Acres	160	Square rods
Acre feet	7758	Barrels
Atmospheres	33.94	Feet of water
Atmospheres	29.92	Inches of mercury
Atmospheres	14.70	Pounds per square inch
Barrels	5.6146	Cubic feet
Barrels	42.0	Gallons
Barrels per hour	.700	Gallons per minute
BTU's per minute	.02356	Horsepower
Centimeters	.3937	Inches
Cubic centimeters	.06102	Cubic inches
Cubic feet	.1781	Barrels
Cubic feet	7.4805	Gallons (US)
Cubic feet of steel	489.6	Pounds of steel
Feet	.3048	Meters

Feet of water @ 60° F	.4331	Pounds per inch
Feet per second	.68182	Miles per hour
Foot-pounds per second	.001818	Horsepower
Gallons (US)	.02381	Barrels
Gallons (US)	.1337	Cubic feet
Gallons (US)	231.0	Cubic inches
Gallons per minute	1.429	Barrels per hour
Grams	.03527	Ounces
Horsepower	33000	Foot-pounds per minute
Horsepower	550	Foot-pounds per second
Horsepower	.7457	Kilowatts
Inches of mercury	1.134	Feet of water
Inches of mercury	.4912	Pounds per square inch
Inches of water @ 60° F	.0361	Pounds per square inch
Kilowatts	1.341	Horsepower
Liters	33.814	Ounces
Liters	1.0567	Quarts
Miles	5280	Feet
Miles per hour	1.4667	Feet per second
Ounces (Avoirdupois)	28.353	Grams
Parts per million	8.337	Pounds per million gallons
Pounds	7000	Grains
Pounds	453.6	Grams
Pounds per square inch	2.309	Feet of water @ 60° F
Pounds per square inch	2.0353	Inches of mercury
Pounds per million gallons	.11982	Parts per million
Pounds per gallons	.1198	Grams per cubic centimeter
Pounds per gallons	.052	Pounds per square inch per ft of depth
Quarts	946.36	Milliliters

Square miles	640	Acres
Tons (long)	2240	Pounds
Tons (short)	2000	Pounds
Yards	.9144	Meters

COMMON EQUIVALENTS

acres X 43,560 = sq ft	cu yd/min X 0.45 = cu ft/sec
acres X 40,471= sq m	cu yd/min X 3.367= gal/sec
atm X 14.7= lb/sq in	cu yd/min X 12.74= 1/sec

bbl oil X 42= gal oil	(F-32) 0.555= C°
bbl X 5.6146= cu ft	Fathoms X 6= ft
bags or sacks of cement X 94	=lb cement

board ft X 144 sq in X lin	= cu in ft X 30.48= cm
C° X 1.8 + 32= F	ft X 0.3048= m
Chair X 66= feet	ft X 0.33333= yd

cm /sec X 1.969= ft/min	ft water X 304.8= kg/sq in
cm /sec X 0.036= km/hr	ft water X 62.43= lb/sq ft
cm /sec X 0.02237= miles/hr	ft water X 0.4335= lb/sq in
cm /sec/sec X 0.03281= ft/sec/sec	

cu ft/ min X 472.0	= u cm/sec ft/min X 0.508= cm/sec

cu ft/ min X 0.1247	= gal/sec ft/min X 0.01667= ft/sec
cu ft/ min X 0.4720	=1/sec ft/min X 0.01829= km/hr
cu ft/ min X 62.43	= lb water/min ft/min X 0.3048= m/min
cu ft/ sec X 0.6463	= million gal/day ft/min X 0.01136= miles/hr
cu ft/ sec X 448.83	= gal/min
cu in X 16.39= cu cm	ft/sec X 30.48= cm/sec
cu in X 0.03463	= pt (liq) ft/sec X 1.097= km/hr
cu in X 0.01732	= qt (liq) ft/sec X 0.5921= knots
	ft/sec X 18.29= m/min
cu m X 35.31= cu ft	ft/sec X 0.6818= miles/hr
cu m X 61.023= cu in	ft/sec X 0.01136= miles/min
cu m X 1.308= cu yd	ft/sec/sec X 30.48 =cm/sec/sec
cu m X 264.2= gal	ft/sec/sec X 0.3048 =m/sec/sec
cu m X 2113= pt (liq)	
cu m X 1057= qt (liq)	Furlongs X 660= ft
cu yd X 7.646 X 10^5= cu cm	gal X 3785= cu/cm
cu yd X 27= cu ft	gal X 0.1337= cu ft
cu yd X 46,656= cu in	gal X 231= cu in
cu yd X 0.7646= cu in	gal X 3.785 X 10^{-3}= cu m
	gal X 4.951 X 10^{-3}= cu yd
cu yd X 202.0=	gal X 3.785= liters

gal X 8= pt (liq)	gal X 4= qt (liq)
cu yd X 764.6=	1
cu yd X 1616=	pt (liq)
cu yd X 807.9=	qt (liq)gal Imperial X 1.20095= gal(US)
	gal (US) X 0.83267= gal Imperial
gal water (US) X 8.3453= lb water	
gal/min X 2.228 X 10⁻³= cu ft/sec	km/hr/sec X 0.9113= ft/sec/sec
gal/min X 0.06308= 1/sec	km/hr/sec X 0.2778= m/sec/sec
gal/min X 8.0208= cu ft/hr	kilowatt X 1.341= hp
gal water/min X 6.0086= tons/day	m X 100= cm
gran (avoir) X 0.0648= grams	m X 3.281= ft
hectare X 2.471= acres	m X 39.37= in
hp X 42.44	= B/minm/min X 1.667= cm/sec
hp X 33,000	= ft-lb/minm/min X 3.281= ft/min
hp X 550= ft-lb/sec	m/min X 0.05468= t/sec
hp X 1.014= hp metric	m/min X 0.06= km/hr
hp-hr X 1.98 X 10⁶= ft-lb	m/min X 0.03728= miles/hr
hp-hr X 0.7457= kw-hr	
in X 2.54= cm	
	m/sec X 196.8= ft/min

in mercury X 0.0334= atm	m/sec X 3.281= ft/sec
in mercury X 0.4912= lb/sq ft	m/sec X 3.6= km/hr
	m/sec X 0.06= km/min
in water X 0.002458= atm	m/sec X 2.237= miles/min
	m/sec X 0.03728= miles/min
in water X 0.07355 =	in hr
in water X 25.4= kg/sq m	miles X 1.069 X 10^5= cm
in water X 5.202= lb/sq ft	miles X 5280= ft
in water X 0.03613 =	lb/sq in miles X1.069= km
	miles X 1760= yd
kg X 980,665=	dynes
kb X 2.205= lb avdp	miles (naut) X 6,080.2= ft
kg X 1.102 X 10^{-3}=	tons (short)
	miles/hr X 44.70 = cm/sec
kg/m X 0.6720= lb/ft	miles/hr X 88= ft/min
kg/sq m X 0.2048 =	lb/sq ft miles/hr X 1.467= ft/sec
kg/sq m X 10^6= kg/sq m	miles/hr X 1.609 = km/hr
	miles/hr X 0.8684 = knots
km X 0.6214= miles	miles/hr X 26.82= m/min
km X 1094= yd miles/ min X 2682= cm/sec	
km/hr X 27.78=	cum/sec miles/min X 88= ft/sec
km/hr X 54.68=	ft/min miles/min X 1.609= km/min

km/hr X 0.9113	=ft/sec miles/min X 60= miles/hr
km/hr X 0.5396	=knots
km/hr X 0.6214	=miles/hr
million gal/day X 1.54723	=cu ft/sec
km/hr/sec X 27.78 =cm/sec/sec	parts/million X 0.0584= grains/US gal
	parts/million X 0.07016= grains/Imperial gal
	parts/million X 8.345= lb/million gal
lb avdp X 16= oz avdp	sq cm X 1.076 X 10^{-3}= sq ft
lb avdp X 256= drams	sq cm X 0.1550= sq in
lb avdp X 7,000= grains	sq cm X 10^{-4}= sq m
lb avdp X 0.0005	= tons (short)
lb avdp X 453.5924= g	sq in X 6.452= sq cm
lb avdp X 1.21528= lb troy	sq in X 6.944 X 10^{-3}= sq ft
lb avdp X 14.5833= oz troy	sq in X 645.2= sq mm
lb troy X 5760= grains	sq km X 247.1= aces
lb troy X 240= dwt troy	sq km X 10.76 X 10^{6}= sq ft
lb troy X 12= oz troy	sq km X 10^{6} = sq m
lb troy X 373.24177= g	sq km X 0.3861= sq mi
lb troy X 0.822857= lb avdp	sq km X 1.196 X10^{6} = sq yd
lb troy X 13.1657= oz avdp	sq m X 2.471 X 10^{-4}= acres

lb water X 0.01602= cu ft	sq m X 10.76= sq ft
lb water X 27.68= cu in	sq m X 3.861 X 10^6= sq ft
lb water X 0.1198= gal US	sq m X 1.55 X 10^{-3}= sq in
	sq miles X 640= acres
lb/cu ft X 0.01602	=g/cu cm sq miles X 27.88 X 10^6= sq ft
lb/cu ft X 16.03	=kg/cu m sq miles X 2.59= sq km
lb/cu ft X 5.787 X 10^{-4}= lb/cu in	sq miles X 3.098 X 10^6= sq yd
lb/cu in X 27.68= g/cu cm	kg/cu m
lb/cu in X 2.768 X 10^{-4} =	sq mm X 0.01= sq cm
lb/cu in X1728= cu ft	sq mm X 1.55 X 10^{-3}= sq in
lb/ ft X 1.488= kg/m	sq yd X 2.066 X 10^{-4}= acres
lb/in X 178.6= g/cm	sq yd X 9= sq ft
	sq yd X 0.8361= sq m
psf X 0.01602= ft water	
psf X 4.883= kg/sq m	tons (long) X 1016= kg
psf X 6.945 X 10^{-3}= psi	tons (long) X 2240= lb avdp
psi X 0.06804= atm	tons (long) X 1.12= tons (short)
psi X 2.307= ft water	tons (metric) X 10^3= kg
psi X 703.1= kg/sq m	tons (metric) X 2205= lb avdp
	tons (short) X 2000= lb avdp

qt (dry) X 67.20 = cu in	tons (short) X 32,000= oz avdp
qt (liq) X 57.75 = cu in	tons (short) X 907.18486= kg
	tons (short) X 2430.56= lb troy
seconds (angle) X 4.848 X 10^{-6} =	radians tons (short) X 0.89287= tons (long)
sq ft X 2.296 X 10^{-5}= acres	tons (short) X 29166.66= oz troy
sq ft X 929.0= sq cm	tons (short) X 0.90718= tons (metric)
sq ft X 144= sq in	tons water/day X 1.3349= cu ft/hr
sq ft X 0.0929= sq m	tons water/day X 83.333= lb water/hr
sq ft X 3.587 X 10^{-8}= sq miles	tons water/day X 0.16643= gal/min

CHAPTER 39

OILFIELD ACRONYMS

These acronyms will give you an edge when you see them being used or hear them in the common jargon used in the oil & gas industry. You will run across many more than are here and some that are listed here, you'll never see again. These acronyms are from all over the world and unless you are international and domestically working in the oil & gas industry, then there is very little chance that you will see all of them. They are in alphabetical order and do not cover all of the acronyms used in the industry.

A

- AADE - American Association of Drilling Engineers
- AAODC - American Association of Oil well Drilling Contractors (superseded by IADC)
- AAV - Annulus Access Valve
- ABAN - Abandonment
- ACHE - Air Cooled Heat Exchanger
- ACOU - Acoustic
- ACQU - Acquisition Log
- ADROC - Advanced Rock Properties Report
- ADT - Applied Drilling Technology, ADT Log
- AFE - Authorization for Expenditure, a process of submitting a business proposal

- AFP - Active Fire Protection
- AGRU - Acid Gas Removal Unit
- AHBDF - Along Hole Below Derrick Floor
- AIRG – Air-gun
- AIRRE – Air-gun Report
- AIT - Array Induction Tool
- AL - Appraisal License
- ALARP - As Low As Reasonably Practicable
- ALC - Vertical Seismic Profile Acoustic Log Calibration Report
- ALR - Acoustic Log Report
- AMDEA - activated Methyldiethanolamine
- AMS - Auxiliary Measurement Service Log
- AMV - Annulus Master Valve
- ANACO - Analysis of Core Logs Report
- ANARE - Analysis Report
- AOF - Absolute Open Flow
- AOFP - Absolute Open Flow Potential
- APD - Application for Permit to Drill
- API - American Petroleum Institute
- APPRE - Appraisal Report
- APS - Active Pipe Support
- ARACL - Array Acoustic Log
- ARESV - Analysis of Reservoir
- ARI - Azimuthally Resistivity Image
- ARRC - Array Acoustic Report
- AS - Array Sonic Processing Log
- ASI - ASI Log
- ASME - American Society of Mechanical Engineers
- ASP - Array Sonic Processing Report
- ASTM - American Society for Testing and Materials
- ASV - Annular Safety Valve
- AV - Annular Velocity or Apparent Viscosity
- AVO - Amplitude Versus Offset (geophysics)
- AWB/V - Annulus Wing Block/Valve (XT)
- AWO - Approval for Well Operation

B

- BBL - barrel
- BBSM - Behavioral Based Safety Management
- BBCF - billion cubic feet (of natural gas)
- BDF - Below Derrick Floor
- BDL - Bit Data Log
- BGL - Borehole Geometry Log
- BGL - Below ground level (used as a datum for depths in a well)
- BGS - British Geological Survey
- BGT - Borehole Geometry Tool
- BGWP - Base of Ground Water Protection
- BHA - Bottom Hole Assembly
- BHC - BHC Gamma Ray Log
- BHCA - BHC Acoustic Log
- BHCS - BHC Sonic Log
- BHCT – Bottom hole Circulating Temperature
- BHL - Borehole Log
- BHP - Bottom Hole Pressure
- BHPRP - Borehole Pressure Report
- BHSRE - Bottom Hole Sampling Report
- BHSS - Borehole Seismic Survey
- BHT – Bottom hole Temperature
- BHTV - Borehole Television Report
- BINXQ - Bond Index Quick look Log
- BIOR – Bio-stratigraphic Range Log
- BIORE – Bio-stratigraphy Study Report
- BIVDL - BI/DK/WF/Casing Collar Locator/Gamma Ray Log
- BLI - Bottom of Logging Interval
- BO - Back Off Log
- BOE - barrel(s) of oil equivalent
- BOED - barrel(s) of oil equivalent per day
- BOEPD - barrel(s) of oil equivalent per day
- BOM - Bill of Materials

- BOP - Blowout Preventer
- BOP - Bottom of Pipe
- BOPD - barrel(s) of oil per day
- BOREH - Borehole Seismic Analysis
- BOTHL - Bottom Hole Locator Log
- BOTTO - Bottom Hole Pressure/Temperature Report
- BPD - barrels per day
- BPH - Barrels Per Hour
- BPFL - Borehole Profile Log
- BPLUG - Baker Plug
- BPV - Back Pressure Valve
- BQL - B/QL Log
- BRPLG - Bridge Plug Log
- BRT - Below Rotary Table (used as a datum for depths in a well)
- BSR - Blind Shear Rams (Blowout Preventer)
- BS&W - Basic Sediments and Water
- BTHL - Bottom Hole Log
- BTU - British Thermal Units
- BUR - Build-Up Rate
- BVO - Ball Valve Operator
- BWD - barrels of water per day (often used in reference to oil production)
- BWPD - barrels of water per day

C

- C&E - Well completion and equipment cost
- C&S - Cased and Suspended
- C1 - Methane
- C2 - Ethane
- C3 - Propane
- C4 - Butane
- C6 - Hexanes
- C7+ - Heavy Hydrocarbon Components
- CA - Core Analysis Log

- CALIL - Caliper Log
- CALOG - Circumferential Acoustic Log
- CALVE - Calibrated Velocity Log Data
- CAPP - Canadian Association of Petroleum Producers
- CART - Cam Actuated Running Tool (Housing Running Tool)
- CAS - Casing Log
- CB - Core Barrel
- CBIL - CBIL Log
- CBL - Cement Bond Log (measurement of casing cement integrity)
- CBM - Choke Bridge Module - XT Choke
- CBM - Conventional Buoy Mooring
- CBM - Coal Bed Methane
- CCHT - Core Chart Log
- CCL - Casing Collar Locator (in perforation or completion operations, the tool provides depths by correlation of the casing string's magnetic anomaly with known casing features)
- CCLP - Casing Collar Locator Perforation
- CCLTP - Casing Collar Locator Through Tubing Plug
- CD - Core Description
- CDATA - Core Data
- CDIS - CDI Synthetic Seismic Log
- CDU - Control Distribution Unit
- CDP - Common Depth Point (geophysics)
- CDP - Comprehensive Drilling Plan
- CDRCL - Compensated Dual Resistivity Cal. Log
- CE - CE Log
- CERE - Cement Remedial Log
- CECAN - CEC Analysis
- CEME - Cement Evaluation
- CET - Cement Evaluation Tool
- CFD - Computational Fluid Dynamics
- CGEL - CG EL Log
- CGL - Core Gamma Log
- CGPH - Core Graph Log

- CGR - Condensate gas ratio
- CGTL - Compact Gas to liquids (production equipment small enough to fit on a ship)
- CHCNC - CHCNC Gamma Ray Casing Collar Locator
- CHDTP - Caliper HDT Playback Log
- CHECK – Check shot and Acoustic Calibration Report
- CHESM - Contractor, Health, Environment and Safety Management
- CHKSR – Check shot Survey Report
- CHKSS – Check shot Survey Log
- CHP - Casing Hanger Pressure
- CHROM – Chromato-log
- CHRT - Casing Hanger Running Tool
- CIBP - Cast Iron Bridge Plug
- CILD - Conduction Log
- CIMV - Chemical Injection Metering Valve
- CITHP - Closed In Tubing Head Pressure (tubing head pressure when the well is shut in)
- CIV - Chemical Injection Valve
- CL - Core Log
- CLG - Core Log and Graph
- CM - Choke Module
- CMP - Common Midpoint (geophysics)
- CMR - CMR Log
- CND - Compensated Neutron Density
- CNFDP - CNFD True Vertical Depth Playback Log
- CNGR - Compensated Neutron Gamma Ray Log
- CNL - Compensated Neutron Log
- CNLFD - CNL/FDC Log
- CNS - Central North Sea
- CNCF - Field Normalized Compensated Neutron Porosity
- COL - Collar Log
- COMAN - Compositional Analysis
- COML - Compaction Log
- COMP - Composite Log
- COMPR - Completion Program Report

- COMPU - Computer Report
- COMRE - Completion Record Log
- CONDE - Condensate Analysis Report
- CONDR - Continuous Directional Log
- CORAN - Core Analysis Report
- CORE - Core Report
- CORG – Core gun Log
- CORIB – Cori-band Log
- CORLG - Correlation Log
- COROR - Core Orientation Report
- COXY - Carbon/Oxygen Log
- CPI separator - Corrugated plate interceptor
- CPI - CPI Log
- CPICB - CPI Cori-band Log
- CPIRE - CPI Report
- CRET - Cement Retainer Setting Log
- CRT - Clamp Replacement Tool
- CSF - Cesium Formate
- CSG - Casing
- CSHN - Cased Hole Neutron Log
- CSI - CSI Log
- CSMT - Core Sampler Tester Log
- CSPG - Canadian Society of Petroleum Geologists
- CST - CST Log
- CSTAK - Core Sample Taken Log
- CSTRE - CST Report
- CSUG - Canadian Society for Unconventional Gas
- CT - Coiled Tubing
- CTD - Coiled Tubing Drilling
- CTCO - Coiled Tubing Clean Out
- CTOD - Crack Tip Opening Displacement
- CTRAC - Cement Tracer Log
- CUT - Cutter Log
- CUTTD - Cuttings Description Report
- CWOR- Completion Work Over Riser
- CYBD – Cyber-bond Log

- CYBLK – Cyber look Log
- CYDIP – Cyber-dip Log
- CYDN - Cyberdon Log
- CYPRO – Cyber-products Log

D

- D&C - Drilling and Completions
- DAC - Dipole Acoustic Log
- DARCI – Darcy-Log
- DAT - Wellhead Housing Drill-Ahead Tool
- DAZD - Dip and Azimuth Display
- DC - Drill Collar(s)
- DCALI - Dual Caliper Log
- DD - Directional Driller or Directional Drilling
- DDBHC - DDBHC Waveform Log
- DDET - Depth Determination Log
- DDM - Derrick Drilling Machine (a.k.a. Top Drive)
- DDNL - Dual Det. Neutron Life Log
- DDPT - Drill Data Plot Log
- DECC - Department for Energy and Climate Change
- DECT - Decay Time
- DEFSU - Definitive Survey Report
- DELTA - Delta-T Log
- DEN - Density Log
- DEPAN - Deposit Analysis Report
- DEPC - Depth Control Log
- DESFL - Deep Induction SFL Log
- DEV - Development Well, Lahee classification
- DEVLG - Deviation Log
- DEXP - D-Exponent Log
- DF - Derrick Floor
- DFR - Drilling Factual Report
- DH - Drilling History
- DHC - Depositional History Curve
- DHSV – Down hole Safety Valve

- DHPTT – Down hole Pressure/Temperature Transducer
- DIBHC - DIS BHC Log
- DIEGR - Dielectric Gamma Ray Log
- DIL - Dual Induction Log
- DILB - Dual Induction BHC Log
- DILL - Dual Induction Latero-log
- DILLS - Dual Induction Log-LSS
- DILSL - Dual Induction Log-SLS
- DIM - Directional Inertia Mechanism
- DINT - Dip Interpretation
- DIP – Dip-meter Log
- DIPAR - Dipole Acoustic Report
- DIPBH – Dip-meter Borehole Log
- DIPFT – Dip-meter Fast Log
- DIPLP - Dip Lithology Pressure Log
- DIPRE – Dip-meter Report
- DIPRM - Dip Removal Log
- DIPSA – Dip-meter Soda Log
- DIPSK – Dip-meter Stick Log
- DIRS - Directional Survey Log
- DIRSU - Directional Survey Report
- DIS - DIS-SLS Log
- DISFL - DISFL DBHC Gamma Ray Log
- DISO - Dual Induction Sonic Log
- DL - Development License
- DLIST - Dip List Log
- DLL - Dual Latero-log
- DLS - Dog-Leg Severity (directional drilling)
- DMA - Dead Man Anchor
- DNHO – Down hole Logging
- DOA - Delegation of Authority
- DOE - Department of Energy
- DOWRE – Down hole Report
- DP - Drill Pipe
- DPDV - Dynamically-Positioned Drilling Vessel
- DPL - Dual Propagation Log

- DPLD - Differential Pressure Levitated Device (or Vehicle)
- DPRES - Dual Propagation Resistivity Log
- DPT - Deeper Pool Test, Lahee classification
- DQLC – Dip-meter Quality Control Log
- DR - Dummy Run Log
- DR - Drilling Report
- DRI - Drift Log
- DRLCT - Drilling Chart
- DRLOG - Drilling Log
- DRLPR - Drilling Proposal/Prognosis.
- DRPG - Drilling Program Report
- DRPRS - Drilling Pressure
- DRREP - Drilling Report
- DRYRE - Drying Report
- DS - Deviation Survey
- DSCAN - DSC Analysis Report
- DSI - Dipole Shear Imager
- DSPT - Cross Plots Log
- DST - Drill Stem Test
- DSTG - DSTG Log
- DSTL - Drill Stem Test Log
- DSTND - Dual Space Thermal Neutron Density Log
- DSTPB - Drill Stem Test True Vertical Depth Playback Log
- DSTR - Drill Stem Test Report
- DSTRE - Drill Stem Test Report
- DSTSM - Drill Stem Test Summary Report
- DSTW - Drill Stem Test Job Report/Works
- DSV - Diving Support Vessel or Drilling Supervisor
- DTI - Department of Trade and Industry
- DTPB - CNT True Vertical Depth Playback Log
- DTT - Depth To Time
- DWOP - Drilling Well on Paper (a theoretical exercise conducted involving the Service provider managers)
- DWQL - Dual Water Quick look Log
- DWSS - Dig Well Seismic Surface Log
- DXC - DXC Pressure Pilot Report

E

- E&A - Exploration and Appraisal
- E&P - Exploration and Production
- ECD - Equivalent Circulating Density
- ECP - External Casing Packer
- ECRD - Electrically Controlled Release Tool
- EDP - Exploration Drilling Program Report
- EDP - Emergency Disconnect Package
- EFR - Engineering Factual Report
- EGMBE - Ethylene Glycol Mono-Butyl Ether
- ELT - Economic Limit Test
- EL - Electric Log
- EM - EMOP Log
- EMOP - EMOP Well Site Processing Log
- EMP - Electromagnetic Propagation Log
- EMW - Equivalent Mud Weight
- EN PI - Enhanced Productivity Index Log
- ENG - Engineering Log
- ENGF - Engineer Factual Report
- ENGPD - Engineering Porosity Data
- ENJ – Enter-jet Log
- EOFL - End of Field Life
- EOR - Enhanced Oil Recovery
- EOW - End Of Well Report
- EPCU - Electrical Power Conditioning Unit
- EPIDORIS - Exploration and Production Integrated Drilling Operations and Reservoir Information System
- EPL - EPL Log
- EPLG - Epilog
- EPLPC - EPL-PCD-SGR Log
- EPT - EPT Log
- EPTNG - EPT-NGT Log
- ER(D) - Extended Reach (Drilling)
- ESD - Emergency Shut-Down
- ESP - Electric Submersible Pump

- ETAP - Eastern Trough Area Project
- ETTD - Electromagnetic Thickness Test
- ETU - Electrical Test Unit
- EVARE - Evaluation Report
- EWR - End Of Well Report
- EXL - or XL, Exploration License)
- EZSV - EZSV Log

F

- FAC - Factual Report
- FACHV - Four Arm Caliper Log
- FANAL - Formation Analysis Sheet Log
- FAT - Factory Acceptance Testing
- FBE - Fusion Bonded Epoxy
- FC - Float Collar
- FCP - Final circulating pressure
- FCVE - F Curve Log
- FDC - Formation Density Log
- FDP - Field Development Plan
- FDS - Functional Design Specification
- FEED - Front End Engineering and Design
- FER - Field Equipment Room
- FEWD - Formation Evaluation While Drilling
- FFAC - Formation Factor Log
- FFM - Full Field Model
- FGEOL - Final Geological Report
- FH - Full Hole tool joint
- FID - Final Investment Decision
- FIL - FIL Log
- FINST - Final Stratigraphic Report
- FINTP - Formation Interpretation
- FIT - Formation Integrity Test
- FIV - Formation Isolation Valve
- FL - F Log
- FLIV – Flow Line Injection Valve

- FLIV – Flow line Isolation Valve
- FLOG - FLOG PHIX RHGX Log
- FLOPR - Flow Profile Report
- FLOT - Flying Lead Orientation Tool
- FLOW - Flow & Buildup Test Report
- FLRA - Field Level Risk Assessment
- FLS - Fluid Sample
- FLT - Fault (geology)
- FMECA - Failure Modes, Effects, and Criticality Analysis
- FMI - Formation Micro-imager Log
- FMP - Formation Micro-scan Report
- FMS - Formation Multi-scan Log
- FMTAN - FMT Analysis Report
- FOSV - Full Opening Safety Valve
- FPIT - Free Point Indicator Tool
- FPL - Flow Analysis Log
- FPLAN - Field Plan Log
- FPSO - Floating Production Storage and Offloading vessel
- FPU - Floating Processing Unit
- FRA - Fracture Log
- FRARE - Fracture Report
- FRES - Final Reserve Report
- FS - Fail Safe (as in FS valve)
- FSB – Flow line Support Base
- FSI - Flawless Start-up Initiative
- FSO - Floating Storage Offloading vessel
- FT - Formation Tester Log
- FTRE - Formation Testing Report
- FULDI - Full Diameter Study Report
- FV - Funnel Viscosity or Float Valve
- FWHP - Flowing Well Head Pressure
- FWKO - Free water knock out
- FWL - Free water level
- FWR - Final Well Report
- FWV - Flow Wing Valve (also known as Production Wing Valve)

G

- GC - Gas Condensate
- GAS - Gas Log
- GASAN - Gas Analysis Report
- GBS - Gravity Based Structure
- GBT - Gravity Base Tank
- GCLOG - Graphic Core Log
- GCT - GCT Log
- GDIP – Geo-dip Log
- GE - Condensate gas equivalent
- GEOCH - Geochemical Evaluation
- GEODY - GEO DYS Log
- GEOEV - Geochemical Evaluation Report
- GEOFO - Geological & Formation Evaluation Report
- GEOL - Geological Surveillance Log
- GEOP - Geophone Data Log
- GEOPN - Geological Well Prognosis Report
- GEOPR - Geological Operations Prognosis Report
- GEORE - Geological Report
- GGRG - Gauge Ring
- GIIP - Gas Initially In Place
- GIS - Geographic Information System
- GL - Gas Lift or Ground Level
- GLM - Gas Lift Mandrel (alternative name for Side Pocket Mandrel)
- GLR - Gas Liquid Ratio
- GLT - GLT Log
- GLV - Gas Lift Valve
- GOC - Gas Oil Contact
- GOM - Gulf of Mexico
- GOP - Geological Operations Report
- GOR - Gas Oil Ratio
- GOSP - Gas/Oil Separation Plant
- GPIT – Inclinometer Tool Log
- GPLT - Geol Plot Log

- GPSL - Geo Pressure Log
- GRAD - Gradiometer Log
- GRLOG – Graph-log
- GRN - Gamma Ray Neutron Log
- GRP - Glass Reinforced Plastic
- GRV - Gross Rock Volume
- GRSVY - Gradient Survey Log
- GST - GST Log
- GTL - Gas to liquids
- GTW - Gas To Wire
- GUN - Gun Set Log
- GWC - Gas-Water Contact
- GWREP - Geo Well Report

H

- HAZID - Hazard Identification (meeting)
- HC - Hydrocarbons
- HCCS - Horizontal Clamp Connection System
- HCM - Horizontal Connection Module. To connect the Xmas Tree to the Manifold
- HDT - High Resolution Dip-meter Log
- HDPE- High Density Poly Ethylene
- HEXT - Hex Dip-log
- HFE - Human Factors Engineering
- HGS - High (specific-)Gravity Solids
- HHP - Hydraulic Horsepower
- HIPPS - High Integrity Pressure Protection System
- HISC - Hydrogen induced stress cracking
- HL - Hook Load
- HLO - Heavy Load-out (Facility)
- HP - Hydrostatic Pressure
- HPGAG - High Pressure Gauge
- HPHT - High Pressure High Temperature (same as HTHP)
- HPPS - HP Pressure Log
- HPU - Hydraulic Power Unit

- HSE - Health, Safety and Environment
- HTHP - High Temperature High Pressure (same as HPHT)
- HVDC - High Voltage Direct Current
- HWDP - Heavy-Weight Drill Pipe
- HUD - Hold Up Depth
- HWDP - Heavy Weight Drill Pipe
- HYPJ – Hyper-jet
- HYROP - Hydrophone Log

I

- I:P - Injector To Producer Ratio
- IADC - International Association of Drilling Contractors
- IBC - Intermediate Bulk Container
- ICOTA - Intervention and Coiled Tubing Association
- ICP - Intermediate Casing Point
- ICSU - Integrated Commissioning and Start Up
- ICV - Interval Control Valve
- ID - Inner or Internal Diameter (of a tubular component such as a casing)
- IDC - Intangible Drilling Costs
- IDEL - IDEL Log
- IEB - Induction Electro BHC Log
- IEL - Induction Electrical Log
- IF - Internal Flush tool joint
- IH - Gamma Ray Log
- IJL - Injection Log
- IL - Induction Log
- ILI – In Line Inspection (Intelligent Pigging)
- ILOGS - Image Logs
- IMAG - Image Analysis Report
- IMCA - International Marine Contractors Association
- INCR - Incline Report
- INCRE - Incline Report
- INDRS - IND RES Sonic Log
- INDT - INDT Log

- INDWE - Individual Well Record Report
- INJEC - Injection Falloff Log
- INSUR – In run Survey Report
- INVES - Investigative Program Report
- IOC - International Oil Company
- IPAA - Independent Petroleum Association of America
- IPC - Installed Production Capacity
- IPLS - IPLS Log
- IPR - Inflow Performance Relationship
- IR - Interpretation Report
- IRTJ - IRTJ Gamma Ray Slim hole Log
- ISF - ISF Sonic Log
- ISFBG - ISF BHC GR Log
- ISFCD - ISF Conductivity Log
- ISFGR - ISF GR Casing Collar Locator Log
- ISFL ISF-LSS Log
- ISFP - ISF Sonic True Vertical Depth Playback Log
- ISFPB - ISF True Vertical Depth Playback Log
- ISFSL - ISF SLS MSFL Log
- ITS - Influx To Surface
- IWCF - International Well Control Federation
- IWOCS- Installation / Work-over Control System

J

- J&A - Junked and abandoned
- JB - Junk Basket
- JU - Jack-Up drilling rig
- JT - Joule-Thomson (effect/valve/separator)
- JVP - Joint Venture Partners/Participants

K

- KOP - Kick-Off Point (directional drilling)
- KOC - Kick Off Plug
- KRP - Kill rate pressure

- KB - Kelly Bushing

L

- LACT - Lease Automatic Custody Transfer
- LAH – Look ahead
- LARS - Launch & Recovery System
- LAT - Lowest Astronomical Tide
- LCM - Lost Circulation Material
- LCNLG - LDT CNL Gamma Ray Log
- LDL - Litho Density Log
- LDTEP - LDT EPT Gamma Ray Log
- LEAKL - Leak Detection Log
- LEPRE - Litho-Elastic Property Report
- LGR - Liquid Gas Ratio
- LGS - Low (specific-)Gravity Solids
- LINCO - Liner and Completion Prognosis. Report
- LIOG - Lithography Log
- LITDE - Litho Density Quick look Log
- LITHR – Litho-logical Description Report
- LITRE – Litho-stratigraphy Report
- LITST – Litho-stratigraphic Log
- LKO - Lowest Known Oil
- LL – Latero-log
- LMAP - Location Map
- LMRP - Lower Marine Riser Package
- LMV - Lower Master Valve (on a Xmas tree)
- LNG - Liquefied Natural Gas
- LOA - Letter of Authorization/Agreement
- LOE - Lease Operating Expenses
- LOGGN - Logging Whilst Drilling
- LOGRS - Log Restoration Report
- LOGSM - Log Sample
- LOLER - Lifting Operations and Lifting Equipment Regulations
- LOT - Leak-Off Test

- LOT - Linear Override Tool
- LOT - Lock Open Tool
- LP - Low Pressure
- LPG - Liquefied Petroleum Gas
- LSBGR - Long Spacing BHC GR Log
- LSSON - Long Spacing Sonic Log
- LT - Linear Time
- LTI(FR) - Lost Time Incident (Frequency Rate)
- LUMI - Luminescence Log
- LVEL - Linear Velocity Log
- LWD - Logging While Drilling

M

- M or m - prefix designating a number in thousands (not to be confused with SI prefix M for mega- or m for milli)
- MAASP - Maximum Acceptable [or Allowable] Annular Shut-in Pressure
- MAC – Multi-pole Acoustic Log
- MACL – Multi-arm Caliper Log
- MAGST – Magneto-stratigraphic Report
- MAOP - Maximum Allowable Operating Pressure
- MARA – Mara-log
- MAWP - Maximum Allowable Working Pressure
- MBD - thousand barrels per day
- MBOD - thousand barrels of oil per day
- MCHE - Main Cryogenic Heat Exchanger
- MCM - Manifold Choke Module
- MCS - Manifold & Connection System
- MCS - Master Control Station
- MD – millidarcy, measure of permeability, with units of area
- MD - Measured Depth (see also MDSS)
- MD - Measurements/Drilling Log
- MDEA - Methyl Di-ethanolamine
- MDL - Methane Drainage License (United Kingdom)

- MDSS - Measured Depth Sub-Sea
- MDT - Modular formation Dynamic Tester
- MEA – Mono-ethanolamine
- MEG - Mono-Ethylene Glycol
- MEPRL - Mechanical Properties Log
- MERCR - Mercury Injection Study Report
- MERG - Merge FDC/CNL/Gamma Ray/Dual Laterolog/ Micro SFL Log
- MEST - MEST Log
- MF - Marsh Funnel (mud viscosity)
- MFCT – Multi finger Caliper Tool
- MGL – Magna-log
- MLH - Mud Liner Hanger
- MIFR - Mini Frac Log
- MINL – Mini-log
- MIPAL - Micropaleo Log
- MIYP - maximum internal yield pressure
- MKB - Meters below Kelly Bushing
- ML – Micro-log
- MLL – Micro-latero-log
- MLF - Marine Loading Facility
- MM or mm - prefix designating a number in millions (not to be confused with SI unit mm for millimeter)
- MMBD - million barrels per day
- MMBOD - million barrels of oil per day
- MMS - Minerals Management Service, (United States)
- MMSCFD - million standard cubic feet per day
- MMTPA - Millions of Metric Tons per Annum
- MMSTB - million stock barrels
- MNP - Merge and Playback Log
- MODU - Mobile Offshore Drilling Unit
- MOF - Marine Offloading Facility
- MOPU - Mobile Offshore Production Unit
- MOT - Materials/Marine Offloading Terminal
- MPA - Micropaleo Analysis Report
- MPD - Managed Pressure Drilling

- MPFM - Multi-Phase Flow Meter
- MPK - Merged Playback Log
- MPQT - Manufacturing Procedure Qualification Test
- MPS - Manufacturing Procedure Specification
- MPV - Multi Purpose Vessel
- MQC - Multi Quick Connection Plate
- MR - Marine Riser
- MRCV - Multi Reverse Circulating Valve
- MRIRE - Magnetic Resonance Image Report
- MSCT - MSCT Gamma Ray Log
- MSFL - Micro SFL Log
- MSL - Mean sea level
- MSL - Micro Spherical Log
- MSS - Magnetic Single Shot
- MST - MST EXP Resistivity Log
- MTT - MTT Multi-Isotope Trace Tool
- MUD - Mud Log
- MUDT - Mud Temperature Log
- MuSol - Mutual Solvent
- MVB - Master Valve Block (XT)
- MWD - Measurement While Drilling
- MWDRE - Measurement While Drilling Report
- MWS - Marine Warranty Survey

N

- NACE - National Association of Corrosion Engineers
- NAPF - Non Aqueous Phase Fluid
- NAVIG - Navigational Log
- NB - Nominal Bore
- NDE - Non Destructive Examination
- NEUT - Neutron Log
- NFI - No Further Investment
- NFW - New Field Wildcat, Lahee classification
- NGDC - National Geo-science Data Centre (United Kingdom)

- NGL - Natural Gas Liquids
- NGR - Natural Gamma Ray
- NGRC - National Geological Records Centre (United Kingdom)
- NGS - NGS Log
- NGSS - NGS Spectra Log
- NGT - NGT Log
- NGTLD - NGT LDT QL Log
- NGLQT - NGT QL Log
- NGTR - NGT Ratio Log
- NHDA - National Hydrocarbons Data Archive
- NHPV - Net Hydrocarbon Pore Volume
- NMHC - Non-Methane Hydrocarbons
- NMVOC - Non-Methane Volatile Organic Compounds
- NNS - Northern North Sea
- NOISL - Noise Log
- NOC - National Oil Company
- NPD - Norwegian Petroleum Directorate, Norway
- NPS - Nominal Pipe Size (sometimes NS)
- NPSH - Net Positive Suction Head
- NPV - Net Present Value
- NRV - Non Return Valve (Chicksan valve that only allows flow in one direction)
- NPW - New Pool Wildcat, Lahee classification
- NS -North Sea
- NTHF - Non-Toxic High Flash
- NTU – Nephelo-metric Turbidity Unit
- NUMAR - Magnetic Resonance Image Log

O

- O&G - Oil and Gas (referring to the industry or the companies in it)
- OBCS- Ocean Bottom Cable System
- OBDTL - OBDT Log
- OBEVA - OBDT Evaluation Report

- OBM - Oil-Based Mud
- OCIMF - Oil Companies International Marine Forum
- OCL - Quality Control Log
- OCTG - Oil Country Tubular Goods (oil well casing, tubing, and drill pipe)
- OD - Outer Diameter (of a tubular component such as casing)
- ODT - Oil Down To
- OFST - Offset Vertical Seismic Profile
- OEM - Original Equipment Manufacturer
- OH – Open hole Log
- OIM - Offshore Installation Manager
- OMRL - OMRL Log
- ONAN - Oil Natural Air Natural cooled transformer
- OOE - Offshore Operation Engineer (senior technical authority on an offshore oil platform)
- OOT - Out of Tolerance
- OPEC - Organization of Petroleum Exporting Countries
- OPL - Operations Log
- OPRES - Overpressure Log
- OPS - Operations Report
- ORICO - Oriented Core Data Report
- OTL - Operations Team Leader
- OWC - Oil Water Contact
- OT - Off Tree
- OUT - Outpost, Lahee classification
- OVCH - Oversize Charts
- OVID - Offshore Vessel Inspection Database
- OWC - Oil-Water Contact

P

- P&A - plugged and abandoned
- PEA - Paleo Environment Study Report
- PADPRT - Pressure Assisted Drill pipe Running Tool
- PAL - Paleo Chart

- PALYN – Paleontological Analysis Report
- PAR - Pre-Assembled Rack
- PAGA - Public Address General Alarm
- PAU - Pre-Assembled Unit
- PBDMS - Playback DMSLS Log
- PBR - Polished Bore Receptacle (component of a completion string)
- PBTD - Plug Back Total Depth
- PBU - Pressure Build Up (applies to integrity testing on valves)
- PCB - Poly Chlorinated Biphenyl
- PCCL - Perforation Casing Collar Locator Log
- PCDM - Power and Control Distribution Module
- PCKR - Packer Log
- PCOLL - Perforation and Collar
- PDC - Perforation Depth Control
- PDC - Polycrystalline Diamond Composite
- PDG - Permanent Down hole Gauge
- PDKL - PDK Log
- PDKR - PDK 100 Report
- PDP - Proved Developed Reserves
- PDNP - Proved Developed Not Producing
- PE - Petroleum Engineer
- PEDL - Petroleum Exploration and Development License
- PENL - Penetration Log
- PEP - PEP Log
- PERDC - Perforation Depth Control
- PERFO - Perforation Log
- PERM - Permeability
- PERML - Permeability Log
- PESBG - Petroleum Exploration Society of Great Britain
- PETA – Petro-graphical Analysis Report
- PETD – Petro-graphic Data Log
- PETLG – Petro-physical Evaluation Log
- PETPM - Petrography Permeametry Report
- PETRP – Petro-physical Evaluation Report

- PFE - Plate/Frame Heat Exchanger
- PFHE - Plate Fin Heat Exchanger
- PLET - Pipeline End Termination
- PFC - PFC Log
- PFPG - Perforation Plug Log
- PFREC - Perforation Record Log
- PG - Pressure Gauge (Report)
- PGB - Permanent Guide Base
- PGOR - Produced Gas Oil Ratio
- PH - Phasor Log
- PHASE - Phasor Processing Log
- PHOL - Photon Log
- PHYFM - Physical Formation Log
- PI - Productivity Index or (Permit Issued)
- PINTL - Production Interpretation
- PIP - Pipe in Pipe
- PL - Production License
- PLEM - Pipeline End Manifold
- PLES -Pipeline End Structure
- PLG - Plug Log
- PLS - Position Location System
- PLT - Production Logging Tool
- PLTQ - Production Logging Tool Quick look Log
- PLTRE - Production Logging Tool Report
- PMI - Positive Material Identification
- PMV -Production Master Valve
- POB - Personnel on Board
- POBM - Pseudo-Oil-Based Mud
- POF - Permanent Operations Facility
- POOH - Pull Out Of Hole
- PON - Petroleum Operations Notice
- POR - Density Porosity Log
- POSFR - Post Fracture Report
- POSTW - Post Well Appraisal Report
- POSWE - Post Well Summary Report
- PP - DXC Pressure Plot Log

- PPCF - Pounds Per Cubic Foot
- PPG - Pounds Per Gallon
- PPI - Post Production Inspection/Intervention
- PPI - Post Pipe lay Installation
- PPTF - Pounds (per square inch) Per Thousand Feet (of depth) - a unit of fluid density/pressure peculiar to Shell
- PPS - Production Packer Setting
- PR2 - Testing regime to API6A Annex F
- PRA - Production Reporting & Allocation
- PREC - Perforation Record
- PRESS - Pressure Report
- PROD - Production Log
- PROTE - Production Test Report
- PROX - Proximity Log
- PRSRE - Pressure Gauge Report
- PSANA - Pressure Analysis
- PSA - Production Sharing Agreement
- PSC - Production Sharing Contract
- PSIA - Pounds Per Square Inch Atmospheric
- PSIG - Pounds Per Square Inch Gauge
- PSL - Product Specification Level
- PSLOG - Pressure Log
- PSP - pseudostatic spontaneous potential
- PSPL - PSP Leak Detection Log
- PSQ - Plug Squeeze Log
- PST - PST Log
- PSV - Pressure Safety Valve
- PSVAL - Pressure Evaluation Log
- PTS - Pipeline Termination Structure
- PTSET - Production Test Setter
- PTTC - Petroleum Technology Transfer Council, United States
- PUD - Proved Undeveloped Reserves
- PUN - Puncher Log
- PUR - Plant Upset Report

- PUWER - Provision and Use of Work Equipment Regulations
- PV - Plastic Viscosity
- PVT - Pressure Volume Temperature
- PVTRE - Pressure Volume Temperature Report
- PW - Produced Water
- PWB - Production Wing Block (XT)
- PWRI - Produced Water Re-Injection
- PWV - Production Wing Valve (also known as a flow wing valve on a Xmas tree)
- PSD - Planned Shut-Down
- PMV - Production Master Valve

Q

- QC - Quality control
- QCR - Quality Control Report
- QL – Quick look Log

R

- RAC - Ratio Curves
- RACI - Responsible / Accountable / Consulted / Informed
- RAM - Reliability, Availability, and Maintainability
- RAWS - Raw Stacks VSP Log
- RBP - Retrievable Bridge Plug
- RKB - Rotary Kelly Bushings
- RCA - Root Cause Analysis
- RCKST - Rig Check shot
- RCD - Rotating Control Device
- RCL - Retainer Correlation Log
- RCM - Reliability Centered Maintenance
- RCR - Remote Component Replacement(Tool)
- RE - Reservoir Engineer
- REOR - Reorientation Log
- RE-PE - Re-Perforation Report

- RESAN - Reservoir Analysis
- RESEV - Reservoir Evaluation
- RESFL - Reservoir Fluid
- RESI - Resistivity Log
- RESL - Reservoir Log
- RESOI - Residual Oil
- REZ - Renewable Energy Zone
- RF - Recovery Factor
- RFLNG - Ready for LNG
- RFMTS - Repeat Formation Tester
- RFSU - Ready For Start-Up
- RFT - Repeat Formation Tester
- RFTRE - Repeat Formation Tester Report
- RFTS - Repeat Formation Tester Sample
- RIGMO - Rig Move
- RIH - Run In Hole
- RITT - Riser Insertion Tube (Tool)
- RKB - Rotary Kelly Bushing (a datum for measuring depth in an oil well)
- RLOF - Rock Load out Facility
- RMLC - Request for Mineral Land Clearance
- RMP - Reservoir Management Plan
- RMS - Ratcheting Mule Shoe
- RNT - RNT Log
- ROCT - Rotary Coring Tool
- ROP - Rate of Penetration
- ROV/WROV - Remotely Operated Vehicle/Work Class Remotely Operated Vehicle , used for subsea construction and maintenance
- ROZ - Recoverable Oil Zone
- ROWS - Remote Operator Workstation
- RPCM - Ring Pair Corrosion Monitoring
- RROCK - Routine Rock Properties Report
- RSS - Rig Site Survey
- RST - Reservoir Saturation Tool (Schlumberger) Log
- RTTS - Retrievable Test-Treat-Squeeze (packer)

- RWD - RWD Log

S

- SABA - Supplied Air Breathing Apparatus
- SAGD - Steam Assisted Gravity Drainage
- SALM - Single Anchor Loading Mooring
- SAM - Subsea Accumulator Module
- SAML - Sample Log
- SAMTK - Sample Taker Log
- SANDA - Sandstone Analysis Log
- SAT - SAT Log
- SAT - Site Acceptance Test
- SB - SIT-BO Log
- SBF - Synthetic Base Fluid
- SBM - Synthetic Base Mud
- SBT - Segmented Bond Tool
- SC - Seismic Calibration
- SCAL - Special core analysis
- SCAP - Scallops Log
- SCBA - Self Contained Breathing Apparatus
- SCDES - Sidewall Core Description
- SCF - Standard cubic feet (of natural gas)
- SCHLL - Schlumberger Log also SCHLO, SCHLU
- SCM(MB) - Subsea Control Module (Mounting Base)
- SCO - Synthetic crude oil
- SCR- Silicon controlled rectifier
- SCRS - Sidewall Cores
- SCSSV - Surface Controlled Subsurface Safety Valve
- SD - Sonic Density
- SDFN - Shut Down For Night
- SDIC - Sonic Dual Induction
- SDL - Supplier Document List
- SDM/U - Subsea Distribution Module/Unit
- SDPBH - SDP Bottom Hole Pressure Report
- SDT - Step Draw-down Test (sometimes SDDT)

- SDU/M - Subsea Distribution Unit/Module
- SEA - Strategic Environmental Assessment (United Kingdom)
- SECGU - Section Gauge Log
- SEDHI - Sedimentary History
- SEDIM - Sedimentology
- SEDL - Sedimentology Log
- SEDRE - Sedimentology Report
- SEM - Subsea Electronics Module
- SEMI (or Semi-Sub) - Semi-Submersible Drilling Rig
- SEPAR - Separator Sampling Report
- SEQSU - Sequential Survey
- SG - Static Gradient
- SGSI - Shell Global Solutions International
- SGUN - Squeeze Gun
- SHA - Sensor Harness Assembly
- SHDT - SHDT Log
- SHO - Stab and Hinge Over
- SHOCK - Shock Log
- SHOWL - Show Log
- SI/TA - Shut In/Temporarily Abandoned
- SICP - Shut-In Casing Pressure
- SIDPP - Shut-In Drill Pipe Pressure
- SIDSM - Sidewall Sample
- SIGTTO - Society of International Gas Tankers and Terminal Operators
- SIMCON - Simultaneous Construction
- SIMOPS - Simultaneous Operations
- SIP - Shut In Pressure
- SIPES - Society of Independent Professional Earth Scientists, United States
- SIT - System Integration Test FR SIT - Field Representation SIT
- SITHP - Shut In Tubing Hanger/Head Pressure (another term for CITHP)
- SITT - Single TT Log

- SIWHP - Shut-in Well Head Pressure
- SKPLT - Stick Plot Log
- SL - Seismic Lines
- SLS - SLS GR Log
- SLT - SLT GR Log
- SMLS - Seamless Pipe
- SNP - Sidewall Neutron Porosity
- SNS - Southern North Sea
- SOBM - Synthetic Oil Based Mud
- SOLAS - Safety of Life at Sea
- SONCB - Sonic Calibration Log
- SONRE - Sonic Calibration Report
- SONWR - Sonic Waveform Report
- SONWV - Sonic Waveform Log
- SP - Shot point (geophysics)
- SP - Spontaneous Potential (Well Log)
- SPCAN - Special core analysis
- SPE - Society of Petroleum Engineers
- SPEAN - Spectral Analysis
- SPEL - Spectralog
- SPFM - Single Phase Flow Meter
- SPH - SPH Log
- SPM - Side Pocket Mandrel or Strokes Per Minute (of a positive-displacement pump)
- SPOP - Spontaneous Potential Log
- SPP - Stand Pipe Pressure
- SPROF - Seismic Profile
- SPS - Subsea Production Systems
- SPT - Shallower Pool Test, Lahee classification
- SQL - Seismic Quick look Log
- SREC - Seismic Record Log
- SRT - Site Receival Test
- SS - Subsea, as in a datum of depth, e.g. TVDSS (true vertical depth subsea)
- SSCP -Subsea Cryogenic Pipeline
- SSCS - Subsea Control System

- SSG - Sidewall Sample Gun
- SSIV - Subsea Isolation Valve
- SSM - Subsea Manifolds
- SSMAR - Synthetic Seismic Marine Log
- SSPLR - Subsea Pig Launcher/Receiver
- SSSL - Supplementary Seismic Survey License
- SSSV - Sub-Surface Safety Valve
- SSTT - Subsea Test Tree
- SSU - Subsea Umbilical
- SSV - Surface Safety Valve
- STAB- Stabilizer
- STAGR - Static Gradient Survey Report
- STB - stock tank barrel
- STC - STC Log
- STFL - Steel Tube Fly Lead
- STGL - Stratigraphic Log
- STIMU - Stimulation Report
- STKPT - Stuck Point
- STL - STL Gamma Ray Log
- STRAT - Stratigraphy, Stratigraphic
- STRRE - Stratigraphy Report
- STOIIP - Stock Tank Oil Initially In Place
- STOP - Safety Training Observation Program
- STSH - String Shot
- SUML - Summarized Log
- SUMRE - Summary Report
- SUMST - Geological Summary Sheet
- SURF - Subsea/Umbilical/Risers/Flow lines
- SURFR - Surface Sampling Report
- SURRE - Survey Report
- SURVL - Survey Chart Log
- SUT(A/B) - Subsea Umbilical Termination (Assembly/Box)
- SWE - Senior Well Engineer
- SWHE - Spiral Wound Heat Exchanger
- SWOT - Strengths, Weaknesses, Opportunities and Threats
- SV - Sleeve Valve

- SYNRE - Synthetic Seismic Report
- SYSEI - Synthetic Seismogram Log

T

- TAGOGR - Thermally Assisted Gas/Oil Gravity Drainage
- TAPLI - Tape Listing
- TAPVE - Tape Verification
- TAR - True Amplitude Recovery
- TB - Tubing Puncher Log
- TBT - Through Bore Tree
- TCA - Total Corrosion Allowance
- TCI - Tungsten Carbide Insert (a type of roller cone drill bit)
- TCF - Temporary Construction Facilities
- TCF - Trillion Cubic Feet(of gas)
- TCPD - Tubing-Conveyed Perforating Depth
- TCU- Thermal Combustion Unit
- TD - Target Depth
- TD - Total Depth)
- TDD - Total Depth (Logger)
- TDL - Total Depth (Driller)
- TDS - Top Drive System
- TDS - Total Dissolved Solids
- TDT - TDT Log
- TDTCP - TDT CPI Log
- TDT GR - TDT Gamma Ray Casing Collar Locator Log
- TEFC - Totally Enclosed Fan Cooled
- TEG - Tri-ethylene Glycol
- TELER – Tidal drift Report
- TEMP- Temperature Log
- TFL - Through Flow Line
- TGB - Temporary Guide Base
- TGOR - Total Gas Oil Ratio (GOR uncorrected for gas lift gas present in the production fluid)
- TH - Tubing Hanger

- THERM - Thermometer Log
- THP - Tubing Hanger Pressure (pressure in the production tubing as measured at the tubing hanger)
- TIE - Tie In Log
- TIW - Texas Iron Works (pressure valve also known as a TIW Trip In With)
- TIEBK - Tieback Report
- TLI - Top of Logging Interval
- TLOG - Technical Log
- TMCM - Transverse Mercator Central Meridian
- TMD - Total Measured Depth in a well-bore
- TNDT - Thermal Neutron Decay Time
- TNDTG - Thermal Neutron Decay Time/Gamma Ray Log
- TOC - Top Of Cement
- TOC - Total Organic Content/Carbon
- TOOH - Trip Out Of Hole
- TOL - Top Of Liner
- TORAN - Torque and Drag Analysis
- TPERF - Tool Performance
- TQM - Total Quality Management
- TRCFR - Total Recordable Case Frequency Rate
- TSA - Thermally Sprayed Aluminum
- TSI - Temporarily Shut In
- TR - Temporary Refuge
- TRA - Tracer Log
- TRACL - Tractor Log
- TRD - Total Report Data
- TREAT - Treatment Report
- TREP - Test Report
- TRIP - Trip Condition Log
- TRSV - Tubing Retrievable Safety Valve
- TRSCSSV - Tubing Retrievable Surface Controlled Sub-Surface Valve
- TRSCSSSV - Tubing Retrievable Surface Controlled Sub-Surface Safety Valve
- TT - Transit Time Log

- TTRD - Through Tubing Rotary Drilling
- TV/BIP - Ratio of Total Volume (ore and overburden) to Bitumen In Place
- TVBDF - True Vertical Depth Below Derrick Floor
- TVD - True Vertical Depth
- TVDPB - True Vertical Depth Playback Log
- TVDSS - True Vertical Depth Sub Sea
- TVELD - Time and Velocity to Depth
- TVRF - True Vertical Depth versus Repeat Formation Tester
- TWT - Two-Way Time (seismic)
- TWTTL - Two-Way Travel Time Log

U

- UBI - Ultrasonic Borehole Imager
- UBIRE - Ultrasonic Borehole Imager Report
- UFJ - Upper Flex Joint
- UGF - Universal Guide Frame
- UIC - Underground Injection Control
- UMCA - Umbilical Midline Connection Assembly
- UMV - Upper Master Valve (from a Xmas tree)
- UPR - Upper Pipe Ram
- URT - Universal Running Tool
- USGS - United States Geological Survey
- UTA - Umbilical Termination Assembly
- UTM - Universal Transverse Mercator

V

- VDENL - Variation Density Log
- VDL - VDL Log
- VDU - Vacuum Distillation Unit, used in processing bitumen
- VELL - Velocity Log
- VERAN - Verticality Analysis

- VERIF - Verification List
- VERLI - Verification Listing
- VERTK - Vertical Thickness
- VIR - Value Investment Ratio
- VISME - Viscosity Measurement
- VIV - Vortex induced Vibration
- VLP - Vertical Lift Performance
- VLTCS - Very Low Temperature Carbon Steel
- VO - Variation Order
- VOCs - Volatile Organic Compounds
- VOR - Variation Order Request
- VRR - Voidage Replacement Ratio
- VSP - Vertical Seismic Profile
- VSPRO - Vertical Seismic Profile
- VTDLL - Vertical Thickness Dual Latero-log
- VTFDC - Vertical Thickness FDC CNL Log
- VTISF - Vertical Thickness ISF Log
- VWL - Velocity Well Log
- VXT -

W

- WABAN - Well Abandonment Report
- WAG - Water Alternating Gas (describes an injection well which alternates between water and gas injection)
- WALKS – Walk away Seismic Profile
- WATAN - Water Analysis
- WAVF - Waveform Log
- WBM - Water-Based Mud
- WC – Water cut
- WE - Well Engineer
- WEG – Wire line Entry Guide
- WELDA - Well Data Report
- WELP - Well Log Plot
- WEQL - Well Equipment Layout
- WESTR - Well Status Record

- WESUR - Well Summary Report
- WFAC - Waveform Acoustic Log
- WGEO - Well Geophone Report
- WGFM - Wet Gas Flow Meter
- WGUNT - Water Gun Test
- WH - Well History
- WHIG - Whitehouse Gauge
- WHP - Wellhead Pressure
- WI - Water Injection
- WI - Working Interest
- WIPSP - WIP Stock Packer
- WLC – Wire line Composite Log
- WLL – Wire line Logging
- WLSUM - Well Summary
- WHM - Wellhead Maintenance
- WHP - Wellhead Pressure
- WOB - Weight On Bit
- WOC - Wait on Cement
- WOE - Well Operations Engineer
- WOM - Wait on Material
- WORKO – Work over
- WOS - West of Shetland, oil province on the UKCS
- WOW - Wait On Weather
- WP - Well Proposal or Working Pressure
- WPLAN - Well Course Plan
- WPQ/S - Weld Procedure Qualification/Specification
- WPR - Well Prognosis Report
- WR – Wire line Retrievable (as in a WR Plug)
- WRS - Well Report Sepia
- WRSCSSV – Wire line Retrievable Surface Controlled Sub-Surface Valve
- WSCL - Well Site Core Log
- WSE - Well Seismic Edit
- WSERE - Well Seismic Edit Report
- WSHT - Well Shoot
- WSL - Well Site Log

- WSO - Water Shut Off
- WSP - Well Seismic Profile
- WSR - Well Shoot Report
- WSS - Well Services Supervisor (leader of Well services at the well site)
- WSSAM - Well Site Sample
- WSSOF - WSS Offset Profile
- WSSUR - Well Seismic Survey Plot
- WSSVP - WSS VSP Raw Shots
- WSSVS - WSS VSP Stacks
- WSTL - Well Site Test Log
- WT - Well Test
- WTI - West Texas Intermediate benchmark crude
- WUT - Water Up To
- WVS - Well Velocity Survey

X

- XL - or EXL, Exploration License
- XLPE -Cross-linked Polyethylene
- XMT - or XT, X-Mas Tree (Christmas Tree, the valve assembly on a production well-head)
- XOM - Exxon Mobil
- XOV - Cross-Over Valve
- XOFC –Cross over Flow Choke

Y

- YF - Holdup Factor
- YP - Yield Point

Z

- Z - Depth, in the geosciences referring to the depth dimension in any x-y-z data.

CHAPTER 40

CLOSING

In the past 26 years of being in the oil & gas industry, I have had the privilege of working with some of the industry's best professionals. I often ask them if they have any words of wisdom to offer a person trying to make it. Some say, "Always remember to keep the pipe moving" Some say, "Never allow an influx into the well-bore" and some just say, "Remember where you started" either saying is correct in my opinion. If we forget where we came from, we treat people differently. If we allow an influx, the well could blow out. If we don't keep the pipe moving, we could get stuck. I am privileged to have had so many opportunities in the oil & gas industry. I feel that this is, and always will be my home.

So in closing, you can see why air hammer drilling is more efficient than its predecessors. It is an all around great application when it can be utilized. It will handle very brittle rock and it works in areas that would make roller cone bits peter out and that would raise your well cost substantially. I am not saying that the roller cone or PDC bits are outlived by any means. They are perfect in the proper applications. In the right application, all bits serve the purpose that they were designed for. But the hammer bit wasn't originally designed to drill oil & gas wells. It was originally designed to drill in the coal mines to help alleviate a lot of the physical labor that was once placed onto the minors as they excavated coal to heat America. We also discussed why down hole motors are a premium tool and what the next step would be in normal circumstances of drilling a well.

These are again only the very basic steps and should not be taken for policy. If you have any questions concerning the proper procedures, refer back to your company's policies and procedures handbook that you should have read upon beginning work. We have discussed several different aspects of an oil & gas well and the steps that it takes to simply complete drilling one. There are so many more steps taken to putting a well online for distribution. The perforating and hydraulic fracing stages would follow this and then the there are even more after those steps. The United States and all of the oil & gas countries are following the same basic steps to drilling an oil or gas well. From Africa to Namibia and Russia to South America, these basic steps are used in the drilling of a well. The permitting process and the safety regulations may differ from country to country and from company to company, but the steps don't change much. So moving forward, learn what you can and mentor others in the fields that you have learned. You never know, the new guy may be your boss down the line.

As we continue to see technology grow and get better, I wouldn't bet even one dollar that the oil & gas people of the world wouldn't be successful at anything that they try. This is a way of life; it will be around until the end of time. When mankind first found oil seeping up from the ground in Pennsylvania, they found an application for it. Entire economies have soared and crashed due to the oil and gas market.

There are some people in the world that believe we need to stop producing oil and gas in the United States and off of our coasts. They believe that it is damaging the environment. I for one have seen disasters in the oil & gas fields, but if we stop drilling for our natural resources, the worst disaster ever witnessed will occur.

In every one of our war waiting opponents' countries, they still explore and produce as much oil & gas as they can possibly get their hands on. What do you think would happen to the US if we ran out of fuel? What if we didn't have the oil & gas to mobilize in the event of an attack? Do you think that the rest of the world would loan us fuel so that we could go to war? I for one believe that if we run out of our natural resources before we have a legitimate replacement, we would become a third world country over night. That would mean; all of the smaller, peaceful countries that depend upon us to protect them would become slave nations. The war loving countries that have waiting for the giant to fall wouldn't hesitate to destroy us and then take the very natural resources that we decided not to produce. That would be a catastrophe wouldn't it? To be enslaved by a country that would force its beliefs upon you and not let you have a choice again. If we stop producing our natural resources, we will fall victim to the tyrants of the world and we will not be ready for the devastation that would follow.

Thank you for your time

Will Pettijohn P.E.C.